THE SUPERSTITIOUS BRIDE

A Book of Wedding Lore

By Rosalind Franklin

British Library Cataloguing In Publication Data

A Record of This Publication is available from the British Library

ISBN 1905363028

First Published in the United Kingdom, June 2005 by Diggory Press, an imprint of Meadow Books, 35 Stonefield Way, Burgess Hill, West Sussex, RH15 8DW, UK

Email: Meadowbooks@hotmail.com
Website: www.diggorypress.com

Other Books by Rosalind Franklin available from Diggory Press

'Baby Lore; Superstitions & Old Wives Tales From The World Over Related to Pregnancy, Birth and Babycare' ISBN 0951565540

INTRODUCTION

I have had lots of fun collecting these wedding related beliefs from all four corners of the globe. Please note that where I have stated the country where a particular belief is held, I'm not inferring the whole nation believes it, neither am I saying that place is the only location where that belief is held. Furthermore, some of the superstitions I have listed are now outdated. For example, the belief that a new Bride was susceptible to fairy abduction, widely accepted as fact up until the beginning of the First World War, now remains only in the memories of our Grandmothers' generation.

However, even where the original *reasons* for the superstitions may have long been forgotten, the *methods* of protection against the feared evils have remained in our culture, staying on in 'quaint' handed down wedding customs. Although of course the modern girl belongs to a far slicker generation than that of her Grandmother, humankind remains the same at its core; inherently fearful and superstitious. Thus although fear of the fairy folk may no longer be an issue, feelings of deep unease and insecurity remain with a wish for 'luck' against intangible dangers. And so along with her 'superstitious' inheritance, *new* Wedding Day customs evolve to be passed down by the modern girl to *her* grandchildren.

Whether you happen to believe or scoff, my hope is that you will enjoy reading this book as much as I have enjoyed putting it together.

Rosalind Franklin, June 2005

INDEX

CHAPTER 1

BEFOREHAND

Omens of a Wedding

~ If a sparrow finds its way into your home, it means someone in your family will marry soon. *Indonesia*

~ It's a good omen if an unmarried woman hears a cock crow when she is thinking of her lover as it predicts an early wedding for her.

~ On May Eve sprinkle ashes on the threshold of the house; if a footprint is found on the threshold in the morning, turned inwards, it predicts marriage. *Pennsylvania: USA* [1]

~ Any dream involving horses is very lucky, and dreaming of a hearse being drawn by white plumed horses is actually a good omen foretelling a wedding. However, dreaming of a wedding itself is very unlucky. *Ireland* [2]

~ A young girl who finds a certain number of horseshoes in a year, or who sees a hundred white horses within the same period, will be married before the year is out. *Germany* [3]

~ A dog sliding on his rump is a sign of a wedding. *Pennsylvania*

~ Put a cat on a mat: the first person the cat approaches out of the group will be the next one to marry. Others say that the first person a cat looks at after washing its face, will get married. *USA*

~ If a man accidentally steps on a cat's tail, he'll marry before the year is through.

~ A young girl will marry the first eligible male she meets on Saint Valentine's Day. *England*

~ If the church bell rings clear, it means a wedding. **Germany** [3]

~ If a woman's neck or throat itches, she'll soon go to a christening or a wedding. **Germany** [4]

~ A woman anxious to get married should feed a cat from her shoe.

The Courtship, Proposal & Engagement

~ A Pair of lovers should never meet at the banks of canals, ponds, bridges, valleys or crossroads; as if they do, love and respect will turn to hatred for each other.

~ Lovers must watch their behaviour at the entrance to each other's homes, as thresholds are the dwelling place of the 'Domovoi', a temperamental brownie spirit who protects the home. Shaking hands or kissing over the threshold is an invasion of the Domovoi's territory and might offend him, bringing bad luck to the household and its occupants. **Russia**

~ For love to run smoothly, never meet each other on the stairs, and certainly never kiss or cuddle there.

~ Engaged people should not be photographed together, else they will soon part, or their marriage will be unhappy.

~ A couple should not look through glass at the new moon together. If they break this rule, they will soon quarrel and one partner will be unfaithful to the other.

~ If love letters are written in pencil or any colour ink other than blue, then the relationship will soon be on the rocks.

~ Three kisses are the luckiest number of kisses to be made at the end of the letter. Four, seven, or thirteen kisses are unlucky.

~ Never drop a letter to your fiancé when you are taking it to the post, as if you do, the next time you meet you'll quarrel.

~ If a man buys or gives his betrothed a book, their love will soon be overturned. ***Germany***[3]

~ Giving yellow flowers means the breaking of bad news or a parting of ways. Carnations of any colour bring unhappiness in love and should never be given to a lover. ***Russia***

~ A man must not give his fiancée a knife or a pair of scissors, lest their love be cut in two. ***Germany***[3]

~ Never give a knife as a present as it is unlucky. ***Russia***

~ It's unlucky to receive a pair of gloves, a brooch or a knife as a gift from a lover, for it means a parting; but it is said that the bad luck may be warded off if a small coin is given in exchange for the gift.

~ Avoid giving handkerchiefs to each other as this will break-up the relationship. ***Indonesia***

~ Never give your loved one a pair of shoes for a Christmas present as this is very unlucky.

~ Never give a cat to a lover, as this will end your relationship.

~ It's unlucky to accept any four-footed animal from your lover. ***Ireland***[2]

~ A violet stone such as the amethyst is always lucky for sweethearts as the violet flower symbolises faithfulness.

~ It's unlucky to accept a lock of hair from a lover. ***Ireland***[2]

~ Possessing a lock of each other's hair, tied into a lovers' knot, assures of lasting affection. ***UK***

~ Love knots are symbols of everlasting love that must never be untied. They are a series of interlacing loops which have no beginning and no end. It is said that in order for either party to move on from a relationship, any love knots must be first untied: otherwise they will always still be 'bound in affection' to the other person. ***England***

~ An engaged couple should give each other carved wooden love spoons decorated with hearts, keys and keyholes, so that they may continually unlock one another's hearts. ***Wales***

~ A broken sixpence, of which the man and woman each keep a piece, ensures they'll never part.

~ Some lovers carry one half each of a 'Mizpah' coin pendant, with the inscription 'The lord watch between thee and me when we are apart' to protect their relationship. ***Jewish***

~ Never get engaged on a Friday. It's a very unlucky day for anything: if you ignore this advice, the malicious fairies will ruin the engagement and marriage for you one way or the other. ***Ireland***

~ The luckiest time for an offer of marriage to be made is on a Friday evening, and the engagement should then be announced on Saturday.

~ If a girl is uncertain as to whether to accept a proposal of marriage, she should place three hairs from a cat's tail into a folded piece of paper under her doorstep. The next morning, the hairs will have formed themselves into a 'Y' or 'N', indicating the correct answer she should give her suitor. ***Ozark Mountains: USA***

~ To discover if her lover will be upright or crooked, a girl must stand against a stack of wood on Christmas Eve and pull a log out backwards; her lover will be like the log. ***Germany***[3]

~ An owl is almost universally taken to be a sign of ill-omen and/or death. Therefore, an owl heard at the time of an announcement of an engagement is a warning sign not to proceed, or a prediction of the early death of one of the partners.

~ If a girl's hair starts to show the first signs of grey when she is engaged, it is a sign that her potential Groom is obviously no good for her and will cause her nothing but lifelong stress!

~ If you marry someone who has been widowed, you too shall die early. One who has been widowed more than once should be avoided like the plague as they must be jinxed.

~ A woman should not marry a man whose surname starts with the same initial as her maiden name as *'Change the name but not the letter, change for worse and not for better.'*

~ If there will be thirteen letters in your new married name, you'll have the devil's luck. Jack the Ripper, Charles Manson, Jeffrey Dahmer, Theodore Bundy and Albert De Salvo all had thirteen letters in their names. If despite this ominous warning, you are still determined to marry your man, perhaps consider adopting a double-barrelled name to prevent this ill-luck. ***USA*** *(See also page 15)*

~ If a suitor rides by horseback to the house where he goes a-wooing, he is careful not to ride a mare else he and his prospective wife will only have daughters. When he arrives at the house, his lady's family quickly undo the saddle straps on his stallion, to facilitate childbirth in the marriage that may come about. ***Estonia*** [3]

~ A man sent members of his family to express his interests to his prospective Bride's family; if, on their way there they saw a blind man, a monk or a pregnant woman, it was immediately assumed the marriage would be doomed. They would thus usually return back home immediately without completing their mission. If, however, they saw nanny goats, pigeons or wolves en-route they rejoiced as these were thought to be good omens that brought good fortune to the marriage.

~ May Day (the festival of 'Beltane') was a very important day to the Ancient Celts. Huge bonfires were lit in honour of 'Bel', the fertile Sun God, and homes were adorned with flowers to bring in the fertilising powers of nature. Other fertility rites such as dancing around the May Pole also took place on this day. May Day was a popular day for proposals of marriage too, as it was believed that the powers 'raised' during this day from the fertility rituals would somehow make a fertile marriage. On the First of May, at the crack of dawn, a man proposed by leaving a hawthorn branch at the door of his beloved. The hawthorn was symbolic of new life to the Celts. If the branch was left at the door, his beloved accepted his proposal, and if she replaced the hawthorn branch with a cauliflower she refused him.

Medieval Brittany

~ The fiancée is given a knife to carry with her at all times until the wedding night to ward off evil spirits and to protect her virtue. *Hindi*

~ A woman should not have sex with a vampire or spirit before marriage as it will make her barren. ***Transylvanian Gypsy*** [18]

~ A man runs off with his beloved. If the woman is pregnant by the time her family catches up with them, the couple is considered married. If she isn't pregnant, her family drag her back home. The couple will run off repeatedly until the 'Bride' conceives, or the woman's mother relents and decides the couple can remain together.

Aborigine: Australia

~ The young people of both sexes cannot enter into a permanent sexual partnership until they have successfully undergone the puberty ordeals, the marriage or the consummation of the marriage following as a direct consequence of surviving such ordeals. The puberty ordeals include: (*a*) rigid fasting, combined with (*b*) exposure to the bites of ants, etc., (*c*) severe scarification, or (*d*) sound flogging - all to be borne without visible signs of suffering to ensure the young people are healthy and strong, willing to work, skilful and industrious.

The Warrau & Carib Indians: Guyana [5]

The Ring

(*See also page 72*)

~ The ring finger follows the vein of love that runs directly to the heart. Since the heart is the seat of love, a ring placed on this finger helps assure the continued love of the spouse for their mate.

Ancient Greece & Rome

~ The engagement ring and wedding ring are worn on the third finger of the left hand as during a Christian wedding, the priest arrives at that finger after touching the thumb and first two fingers on the left hand counting, '... in the name of the Father, the Son and the Holy Ghost'. ***17th Century Europe***

~ A plain gold ring is a never-ending circle of love, and in Victorian times was considered highly suitable as an engagement ring for this reason. ***UK***

~ A gold love knot ring symbolises eternal love, and 'ties' the couple together for always. ***UK***

~ 'Gypsy rings' (rings containing gems set in a row that spell out a word by the first letter of each stone representing the first letter of the word) were very popular in the mid 1800's. The rings were often thought to be lucky and endowed with supernatural power to 'bless' the relationship. Popular words spelled on Gypsy rings were 'Love', 'Amour', 'Amite', and 'Regard'. ***UK***

~ The fire of a diamond reflects the flame of love, and is made from the actual teardrops of the gods. ***Ancient Greece***

~ Diamonds are splinters from falling stars that tip the arrows of Eros, the god of love. ***Ancient Rome***

~ Diamonds have magical properties such as the power to reunite estranged marriage partners. ***Middle Ages: Europe***

~ A diamond, as it is the hardest of all stones, represents eternity and a love that will last forever. ***15ᵗʰ Century Venice***

~ With its translucent qualities and its clear sides and edges, the diamond represents innocence.

~ Opals and pearls should not be set into rings as they bring bad luck and tears.

~ Emeralds represent jealousy and are unlucky, hence the expression 'Green with envy.' ***UK***

~ Sapphires and rubies mean good fortune as they symbolise warm affection and immortal life.

~ Turquoise is the luckiest stone for lovers.

~ Blue stones protect a marriage as they ward off witchcraft and deflect the power of the 'Evil Eye' ***Ancient Egyptian & Modern Mediterranean & Islamic belief***

~ A violet stone such as the amethyst is lucky, symbolising faithfulness.

~ Red stones enhance fertility. ***Ancient Jewish***

~ A man should never ever wear an engagement ring: if he does wear one, he will be hen-pecked and stifled within his marriage. ***UK***

~ To lose an engagement ring foretells a break-up.

~ If the engagement or wedding ring does not fit properly first time, the marriage is not meant to be.

~ A loose ring indicates a 'loose' partner, a tight ring, a constricting and stifling marriage.

~ It's very unlucky to try on a wedding ring before the ceremony, as it may result in a sudden termination of the engagement or an unhappy marriage.

Name Numerology

Letters of the alphabet are said to have a vibratory frequency that can be matched with the vibratory frequency of numbers. Therefore, each letter of the alphabet is given a numerical value. Before choosing their marital name and/or partner, some will check their prospective new name's to see if it's 'fitting'. If the new name number is not fitting, all is not lost as perhaps the marital name can be numerologically tweaked by making the surname double-barrelled to give a better name number.

To calculate the name's numerological value, the full name (i.e.: including any middle names) needs to be used. The table on the following page shows the numerological value assigned to each of the letters in the alphabet. Add the numbers assigned to each of the letters of each of your names together until a single digit figure is achieved. If the number 11 or 22 is reached in the calculations, do not reduce these figures further as they are viewed as numerological 'master' numbers.

1	2	3	4	5	6	7	8	9
A	B	C	D	E	F	G	H	I
J	K	L	M	N	O	P	Q	R
S	T	U	V	W	X	Y	Z	

Example of prospective Name: MARY SALLY JONES

MARY = 4 + 1 + 9 + 7 = 21 = 2 + 1 = 3
SALLY = 1 + 1 + 3 + 3 + 7 = 15 = 1 + 5 = 6
JONES = 1 + 6 + 5 + 5 + 1 = 18 = 1 + 8 = 9

Mary's new name number is therefore calculated as 3 + 6 + 9 = 18
18 reduces to 9. (1+8 = 9)

Mary's new name Number is therefore 9

THE MEANING OF THE NUMBERS

NB. The 'negative' energies attached to a number are not always negative and can make-up for some of a woman's inherent birth weaknesses (believed to be caused by a weak birth name). So for example, if a woman is naturally timid and fearful then Number 1 energy should not be viewed negatively as it will be enhancing for her. However, if a woman is already fiercely independent, extra Number 1 energy will make her become an unbearable dictator within the marriage.

1. Tendency to dominate and to want to be 'Number One'. Ambitious, determined, courageous, independent, egotistical, critical, impatient of trifles, aggressive and very hard to live with. If the husband is a number 1 as well then this makes for a continual clash of wills within a difficult marriage.

2. Diplomatic, tactful, co-operative, easygoing, friendly, sensitive, considerate, affectionate, and persuasive but in a very quiet way. If the husband is a 2 as well then the couple will lack direction and 'drift' through life and be too easygoing for their own good.

3. Eloquent, creative, intuitive, enthusiastically enjoying life to the full. 3's are normally inspiring and motivating, with an active social life. If the husband is a number 3 as well, however, the Bride and or/couple will be superficial with scattered energies.

4. Solid, dependable, predictable, down-to-earth, organised, serious and conscientious. If the husband is a number 4 as well, the Bride and or/couple will become rather boring and inflexible, with a tendency to hide their feelings, or not even be aware of their true feelings.

5. Multi-talented, adventurous, analytical, good at knowing how to approach people to get what is wanted. If the husband is a number 5 as well, the Bride and or/couple will be restless, impatient and erratic. They will have a hard time with routine and tend to jump from activity to activity and place to place without finishing anything.

6: Altruistic, generous, emotional, sympathetic, very giving of love and support. If the husband is a number 6 as well, the Bride and or/couple will become overly meddling and interfering, repressing their own needs for the welfare of others.

7.   Studious, idealistic, introspective, mystical, on a different wavelength. Neither show nor understand emotions very well. Don't easily adapt to new environments or people. If the husband is a number 7 as well, the Bride and or/couple will become too introverted, self-centred, critical and intolerant.

8.   Ambitious, goal-oriented, determined, confident, energetic. Considerable achievement in business or other powerful positions. If the husband is a number 8 as well, the Bride and or/couple can become too materialistic and wrapped up in work and money.

9.   Sensitive, intuitive, compassionate, generous, the selfless humanitarian. 9's have an idealistic and inspirational approach to life. If the husband is a number 9 as well, the Bride and or/couple become too sensitive, feel let down easily and will resent giving all the time.

11.   The first of the numerological master numbers associated with idealistic spiritual issues. Intuitive, inspiring, religiously devoted, the ability to lead people merely by example. If the husband is a number 11 as well, the Bride and or/couple become impractical, lack wisdom and achieve little as they talk rather than do anything.

22.   The master builder. Perceptive and idealistic strong leader, with a broad outlook and common sense. Extremely capable at anything, being especially equipped to handle large-scale undertakings. Well respected with charisma to attract a following. If the husband is a number 22 as well, the Bride and or/couple become dominating, overbearing, and a tad eccentric.

* * * * * *

The Weeks Leading up to the Wedding Day

~ The Bride should not practice writing her new name before her wedding day as it tempts fate. *USA*

~ The Bride mustn't allow her married name to be used in any way before the wedding as it's bad luck. *England*

~ Brides must not read the whole of the wedding ceremony before the Big Day, lest the wedding not come about.

~ The couple should not be present at the first bidding of the banns or they will jinx their marriage. *Germany* [3]

~ At the ball which the Bride is expected to give on the day when her banns are published for the first time, all the guests arrive with nuts in both their hands to salute her with. This links back to ancient fertility rituals. *The Netherlands* [6]

~ Altar-bound couples are accident-prone and therefore must avoid taking long trips for their own safety. *The Philippines*

~ The female is possessed by some evil Spirit, whose influence has to be counteracted and destroyed. Therefore the piai (witch doctor) blows on and mutters over the girl and her more valuable belongings to disenchant her and everything she has come into contact with before her wedding. *Makusi Indians: Guyana* [5]

~ Be very careful who you tell about your engagement and wedding plans, as if the fairies get wind of your activities by overhearing people talking, they will do their utmost to try and ruin things. *Orkney Isles*

~ The first gift the Bride opens at her Bridal Shower or on her Hen Night should be the first gift she uses within the marriage. *USA & UK*

~ Every word that the Bride says as she opens her gifts at her Bridal

Shower will be repeated on her wedding night, albeit under totally different circumstances. ***USA***

~ The person who gives the third gift to be opened at a Bridal Shower will have a baby within a year. ***USA***

~ Save the ribbons from the Bridal Shower gifts to make a mock bouquet to be used at the wedding rehearsal for luck. ***USA***

~ A week before the wedding, the Bride and seven married female members of her family make small balls of *'chana dal'* (lentils), which are later dried and sent to the Groom's house to ensure that the newlywed's pantry is always full of things to eat. ***Asia***

~ A magician sprinkles the earth with yellow rice and rice paste, and offers betel to placate the spirits of the soil on the couple's behalf. Likewise, rice is scattered in water with appeals to all the spirits of water for their blessing. ***Malaysia***

~ If the Bride sneezes on the morning of the day before her wedding, she will have a happy marriage. ***Russia***

~ If there is a full moon one to two days before the wedding day, the marriage will be full of luck.

~ On the strike of midnight on the eve of the wedding, young women gathered in the Bride's home to make periwinkle wreaths. Widows were not permitted to witness the wreath making as it was unlucky. As the Bridesmaids made the wreaths they sang:

> *'Periwinkle, periwinkle, I love to wear thee,*
> *But because of a young man I must leave thee.'*

The Maid of Honour then took each wreath and placed it on bread that was to be used in the wedding proceedings. She then made three complete dance revolutions in the centre of the room for luck. ***Russia***

~ It is very bad luck for the Groom to see the Bride in her Wedding Dress before they are married. *Europe*

~ The Groom should never see his Bride on the night before the wedding or the marriage will fail. Likewise, the Bride and Groom must not see each other on the morning of the wedding day. This superstition perhaps dates to the time of arranged marriages, when the Father of the Bride feared the Groom would flee if his fiancée was not to his liking. Therefore the 'unveiling' was postponed until the actual wedding ceremony.

~ The Bride's father, on the eve before his daughter leaves him, takes sugarcane from the marsh, chews it, and spits its juice onto his daughter's stomach. The sugarcane symbolises children, and is also placed under the marital bed as a fertility charm. *The Democratic Republic of Congo* [+]

~ If the Bride dreams of the face of another man on the night before her wedding, it is an omen that she is marrying the wrong man.

~ Before the wedding, locks of hair were given to placate the goddess Artemis, who was associated with menstruation and childbirth. *Ancient Greece*

~ The Bride-to-be is given a pre-wedding dish of wheat to bless her fertility. *Czech Republic*

~ All knots must be untied before the wedding ceremony to bring about a fertile marriage. *Scotland*

CHAPTER 2

SETTING THE DATE

Wedding Time

~ A postponed wedding, regardless of the reason, is always a bad omen.

~ If a clergyman marries two couples on the same day, one of the couples will be unhappy.

~ If two marriages are celebrated simultaneously, one of the husbands will soon die. **New Orleans: USA** [7]

~ It's bad luck for two siblings to marry during the same year as each other. **The Philippines**

~ Sisters should never marry on the same day, or even during the same year, lest this action condemn them both to unhappy marriages.

~ Never get married at the time of a solar or lunar eclipse as it is an incredibly unlucky time. **India**

~ It is unlucky to get married between two annual religious festivals that are two months apart. **Turkey**

Days to Marry

Monday for wealth,
Tuesday for health,
Wednesday the best day of all.
Thursday for losses,
Friday for crosses,
And Saturday no luck at all. **Traditional Rhyme**

~ The first days of the year and of the week are the luckiest for everything. *Ireland* [2]

~ Those who marry on a Monday or Tuesday will live in poverty. *UK*

~ Tuesday is ruled by Mars, the god of War; if married on this day, Mars' influence will cause continual marital strife.

~ Wednesday is ruled by Wotan, the god often associated with misery. Hence the rhyme 'Wednesday's child is full of woe'. *Europe*

~ On Wednesday, nobody should get married. *Germany* [3]

~ Wednesday and Friday are unlucky days, and Wednesday is never chosen for a wedding. *Alsace: France* [4]

~ Thursday is an unlucky day to marry. *UK*

~ It is on Fridays that the fairies have the most power to work evil; therefore Friday is an unlucky day to have a wedding; for the spirits are then present everywhere, and hear and see everything that is going on, and will mar and spoil all they can, just out of jealousy of the mortal race. *Ireland* [2]

~ It's unlucky to be married on a Friday; especially on a Friday the 13th.

~ Friday has evil associations as it was the day of Jesus' crucifixion, and also, according to tradition, the day on which Adam and Eve ate the forbidden fruit that led to their banishment from Paradise.

~ All Fridays are holy because of their association with Good Friday, and consequently a marriage begun then is likely to be happy.

~ Friday is sacred to Freya (the goddess associated with love and fertility) and so is a lucky day for lovers and weddings. *Scandinavia*

~ The Caithness district was unusual in that Friday was a popular day for weddings whilst elsewhere it was thought unlucky. The reason may have been that weddings always had to end at midnight on Saturday (i.e.: for the Sabbath) and if they were held on Friday one did not have to provide such a large feast! *Scotland*

~ It's unlucky to marry on a Saturday. *Ireland*

~ Saturday was greatly disliked as a marriage on that day would lead to the early death of either the Bride or the Groom. *UK*

~ Saturday is ruled by Saturn, an unlucky and hard, unyielding planet associated with negative energies such as jealousy.

~ The day of the week on which the previous Christmas had fallen must be carefully avoided. The sinister influence of that day affects every corresponding weekday throughout the year that follows.

~ Christmas Day is an unfortunate day for any enterprise, including marriage. *Europe*

Other Things To Consider When Setting The Date

~ Always marry on the upswing of the clock (anytime after half past the hour) as that way the hands of the clock will always be on their way upwards to bring luck to the marriage.

~ Lent is an inappropriate time for a wedding as it should be a time of abstinence. A marriage celebrated then will not have God's blessing. *'Marry in Lent, live to repent.'*

~ Advent and Easter Week (except when they fall in the month of May) were included in the Church's prohibited marriage seasons, as laid down in the Sarum Missal. Before the Reformation, the rule forbidding marriages then was strictly enforced, and a marriage celebrated without special permission during such seasons was thought to be tempting Providence, and unlikely to bring happiness to those concerned. Certain other Church holy days are also ill-omened.

~ Maundy Thursday is an unlucky day in itself as well as being part of the generally unlucky Holy Week.

~ Any Summer month *apart from* the month of May is a good time to marry because of the sun's association with fertility. **UK**

~ Those who marry at harvest time will spend all their lives gathering. **Ireland**

~ Those who marry in autumn will die in the spring. **Ireland** [2]

~ Favourite times for weddings are after the harvest or after the season of rice planting, not only because those are days of leisure but probably so that the baby that is likely to develop within the new Bride's womb will develop simultaneously with the grain planted in Mother Earth. **Malaysia** [8]

~ According to fishermen, it brings bad luck and infertility to get married when the fish aren't biting. **Scotland & Cornwall**

The Moon Cycles

~ As the moon moves in twenty nine day cycles, it became associated with the female menstruation cycle, fertility and childbirth. Most ancient culture's goddesses of fertility are all strongly associated with the moon (e.g.: Greek, Roman, & Aztec). The crescent moon lunar phase is said to be the best time to conceive. The horseshoe symbolises the crescent moon, which is perhaps why it came to be used in wedding ceremonies as a fertility charm.

~ The day of the full moon is the luckiest time for the wedding ceremony. **Ancient Greece**

~ Let a wedding be at full-moon, or the marriage is not blessed.

~ Marriages should take place at the time of the new moon. **Estonia** [3]

~ If you marry at the time of the moon's waning, your good luck will wane also. **Cornwall**

~ The moon has phallic overtones. In ancient symbolism, the horns of the moon were synonymous with the horns of the ox - the ox symbolic of productiveness and fertility.

> *'Pray to the Moon when she is round,*
>
> *Luck with you will then abound,*
>
> *What you seek for shall be found,*
>
> *On the sea or solid ground.'* **Romany Gypsy** [18]

~ It's unlucky to marry during the waning of the moon because the marriage will be childless. Ideally, marry during the waxing phase of the moon, 'when the moon grows and the tide flows'. **Orkney Isles** [9]

Months To Wed

'Marry when the year is new, always loving, always true,

When February Birds do mate, you may wed or dread your fate

If you wed when March winds blow, joy and sorrow both you'll know

Marry in April when you can, joy for maiden and for man,

Marry in the month of May, you will surely rue the day,

Marry when June roses blow, over land and sea you'll go,

They who in July do wed, must labour always for their bread,

Whoever wed in August be, many a change are sure to see,

Marry in September's shine, your living will be rich and fine,

If in October you do marry, love will come but riches tarry,

If you wed in bleak November, only Joy will come, remember,

When December snows fall fast, marry and true love will last.' **UK**

~ January is Hera's month, the Protectress of Wives and Fertility. January was thus a popular time for weddings. ***Ancient Greece***

~ In most Churches the end of April was a busy time for weddings as couples wanted to avoid being married in unlucky May. Queen Victoria forbad her children from marrying in May. ***UK***

~ The men of Rome did not take wives in May as May was the month when offerings were made to the dead during the Feast of the Dead and mourning clothes were worn. The festival of the Goddess of Chastity also occurred in May. ***Ancient Rome***

~ May is an unlucky month to marry in as this was the month in which the Celtic festival of Beltaine occurred with its outdoor orgies. It was thus thought to be an unsuitable time to start married life. ***UK***

~ All women marrying in May will be childless; or, if they have children, their firstborn will be an idiot, or have some physical deformity. ***UK***[10]

~ May marriages are bad as *'All the bairns die and decay.'* ***Scotland***

~ If you marry in May, in a very short time you will grow weary of each other. ***UK***[10]

~ *'Marry in May, rue for aye'* or *'Marry in May and you'll surely rue the day.'* ***UK***

~ June's namesake is Juno, the goddess of woman (who resides over childbirth). She blesses all marriages taking place in her month. ***Ancient Rome***

~ September is lucky as *'Marry in September's shrine, your living will be rich and fine.'* ***UK***

Chinese Astrology

~ The Ox rules January. Therefore it is lucky for a person born in the year of the Ox to marry in this month. The ox's energy makes a dependable albeit stubborn spouse.

~ The Tiger rules February and so Tigers should marry in this month. The Tiger's energy makes a charismatic, brave, warm-hearted spouse albeit prone to mood swings.

~ The Rabbit rules March and Rabbits should marry in this month. Shy and submissive, taking pride in their homes and appearance, rabbits easily stray sexually.

~ The Dragon rules April and Dragons should marry in this month. Aggressive, dominant and the centre of attention, Dragons are very lucky in relationships.

~ The Snake rules the month of May and Snakes should marry in this month. They make charming, seductive, generous, jealous and insecure spouses.

~ The Horse rules June and Horses should marry in this month. However, they don't settle easily and are always roaming from one relationship, job, project or place to another.

~ The Ram (Sheep) rules July and Rams should marry in this month. Bossy, disorganised, indecisive, needing plenty of time alone, Rams often withdraw into a shell, and need plenty of love and reassurance.

~ The Monkey rules the month of August and Monkeys should marry during this month. Monkeys are fun, natural entertainers, very sexy albeit self-centred with little self-control.

~ The Rooster rules September and Roosters should marry in this month. Rather conservative, Roosters dislike risk taking. They expect to be in control, especially over their appearance and of their surroundings.

~ The Dog rules the month of October and Dogs should marry in this month. Dogs are loyal, honest, wise, ethical, perfectionist, intuitive, anxious and insecure.

- The Boar rules November and Boars should marry in this month. Sweet natured, caring a great deal about others, Boars work hard to keep everyone happy. Can be walked over though by others taking advantage of their rose-tinted views.

~The Rat rules December and Rats should marry in this month. They make rather selfish & materialistic spouses.

Specific Dates Of The Year

~ In the Roman calendar, several days are marked as forbidden or unfit for marriages: i.e.: Jan. 24th, Feb. 11th, June 2nd, Sept. 16th, Nov. 2nd, and Dec. 1st. [10]

~ On the days in February known collectively as *The Parentalia*, no temples were allowed to be open, no fire burnt on their altars, and no marriages were allowed to be performed. ***Ancient Rome*** [11]

~ August 24th, October 5th and November 8th were termed *dies religiosi.* On these days the spirits of the dead were believed to come forth into the upper world through the mundus (an entrance to a vault in the city of Romulus which was believed to be the gate of hell). On these days, no public business might be undertaken, no battle fought, no army conscripted, or wedding performed.

Ancient Rome [11]

~ Lucky days: Jan. 14th, April 3rd, May 22nd. Unlucky days: Jan. 21st, April 29th. ***Gloucestershire: UK*** [10]

~ The following days are good to marry or get engaged:

January 2, 4, 11, 19, and 21.

Feb. 1, 3, 10, 19, 21.

March 3, 5, 12, 20, 23.

April 2, 4, 12, 20, and 22.

May, 2, 4, 12, 20, 23.

June 1, 3, 11, 19, 21.

July 1, 3, 12, 19, 21, 31.

August 2, 11, 18, 20, 30.

Sept. 1, 9, 16, 18. 28.

Oct. 1, 8, 15, 17, 27, 29.

Nov. 5, 11, 13, 22, 25.

Dec. 1, 8, 10, 19, 23, 29.' [10]

~ Those who get engaged or marry on the following unlucky days become very poor and miserable:

January 1, 2, 3, 4, 6, 11, 12.

February 1, 17, 18.

March 14,16.

April 10, 17, 18.

May 7, 8.

June 17.

July 17, 21.

August 20, 21.

September 10, 18.

October 6.

November 6, 10.

December 6, 11, 15. *Germany* [24]

~ The unlucky Days according to the opinion of some Astronomers;

January 1, 2, 4, 5, 10, 15, 17, 29, very unlucky

February 26, 27, 28, unlucky; 8, 10, 17, very unlucky

March 16, 17, 20 very unlucky

April 7, 8, 10, 20 unlucky; 16, 21, very unlucky

May 3, 6, unlucky; 7, 15, 20, very unlucky.

June 10, 22, unlucky; 4, 8, very unlucky

July 15, 21, very unlucky

August 1, 29, 30, unlucky; 19, 20, very unlucky

September 3, 4, 21, 23, unlucky; 6, 7, very unlucky

October 4, 16, 24, unlucky; 6 very unlucky

November 5, 6, 29, 30, unlucky; 15, 20, very unlucky

December, 15, 22, unlucky; 6, 7, 9, very unlucky. [12]

~ The thirteenth of any month is always unlucky. *Europe*

~ December 21st is unlucky as any Bride marrying then will soon be a widow. *Yorkshire: UK*

~ December 21st is lucky because as it is the shortest day in the year it 'leaves less time for repentance.' (i.e.: the Bride and Groom will be less likely to repent of their marriage later on!) *Lincolnshire: UK*

Wedding Date Numerology

The Marriage Number is calculated numerologically from the wedding date and represents the energy the couple will carry with them through their married life. As the Birth Date and Life Path Numbers (discovered through dates of birth and birth names) are far stronger influences, the marriage number has a comparatively small effect. However, many believe that effect is still significant enough to pick ones' dates accordingly.

To calculate the Marriage Number, convert the date of marriage to a single digit, from the sum of the day, month and year.

E.g.: If the wedding is on September 28th, 2004:

Add the day 28 ($2+8 = 10 = 1+0 = 1$)

to the month (**9**) to the year 2004 ($2+0+0+4 = 6$)

$= 1+9+6 = 16 = 1 + 6 = 7$

The marriage number is therefore 7.

The Meaning of The Marriage Numbers

1. Ruled by the Sun

An excellent time for marriage as the Sun's influence makes for a successful and fertile marriage.

Yellow is a good colour to wear on the day or to decorate the marital home with, and the couple should surround themselves with gold for luck.

2. Ruled by the Moon

The moon's energy blesses fertility and the couple's feminine and spiritual aspects. However it can make for a moody couple.

Good Colours: white, grey, silver

Elements: silver, moonstone

3. Ruled by Jupiter

Jupiter's energy makes a generous couple who will enjoy riches.

Good Colours: grey

Element: tin

♃. **Ruled by Uranus**

Uranus will create a couple who like to challenge the norm.

Good colours: electric blues and electric pinks

Element: quartz

♄. **Ruled by Mercury**

This couple will be good at communicating with each other.

Good colours: shiny and shimmering colours

Elements: Mercury, electrum

6. **Ruled by Venus**

Venus creates a very romantic, sexy, possibly even over-sexed couple.

Good colours: turquoise, pink,

Elements: Copper, rose quartz, turquoise

7. **Ruled by Neptune**

Neptune creates two withdrawn, uncooperative individuals in a couple

Colours: green

Elements: jade, bloodstone

8. **Ruled by Saturn**

The worst day to marry on! Saturn creates bad luck and loneliness, and the couple will face much opposition and difficulty in life.

Colours: black, dark purple, jet.

Elements: Lead

9. **Ruled by Mars**

Another terrible time to marry as Mars creates warlike, aggressive, argumentative people.

Colours: maroon

Elements: iron

Planetary Hours

If you want to find the ruling planet as per the marriage hour, calculate this from the following tables. (All the planet's energies will be the same as per the qualities given on the previous page under numerology.) Calculate the ruling planet by finding when sunrise is on that day. So for example, if sunrise at the place of marriage is at 5.30am, then between 5.30am and 6.29am is the first planetary hour, 6.30am until 7.29am the second planetary hour and so on.

Looking at the chart, we find that if married on Tuesday at 10.45am, that hour is ruled by Saturn.

Daylight hours - from Sunrise to Sunset - the first hour of sunrise is ruled by the 'Hour 1' listed planet for that day and so on

HOUR	Sunday	Mon.	Tues	Wednesday	Thurs.	Friday	Saturday
1	Sun	Moon	Mars	Mercury	Jupiter	Venus	Saturn
2	Venus	Saturn	Sun	Moon	Mars	Mercury	Jupiter
3	Mercury	Jupiter	Venus	Saturn	Sun	Moon	Mars
4	Moon	Mars	Mercury	Jupiter	Venus	Saturn	Sun
5	Saturn	Sun	Moon	Mars	Mercury	Jupiter	Venus
6	Jupiter	Venus	*Saturn*	Sun	Moon	Mars	Mercury
7	Mars	Mercury	Jupiter	Venus	Saturn	Sun	Moon
8	Sun	Moon	Mars	Mercury	Jupiter	Venus	Saturn
9	Venus	Saturn	Sun	Moon	Mars	Mercury	Jupiter
10	Mercury	Jupiter	Venus	Saturn	Sun	Moon	Mars
11	Moon	Mars	Mercury	Jupiter	Venus	Saturn	Sun
12	Saturn	Sun	Moon	Mars	Mercury	Jupiter	Venus

CHAPTER 3

WEDDING CLOTHES

The Dress

~ The Dress must not have a bird design on it, as this is unlucky.

~ It's unlucky for the Bride to make her own wedding dress.

~ In order to ensure marital bliss, the bridal trousseau (except the gown) should be cut out and sewn by the Bride herself. However some folk disagree and say that the Bride will have no luck if she makes her own trousseau.

~ Never cut out a dress or begin to make it on a Friday as it is unlucky. *Ireland*[2]

~ A second-hand wedding Dress may be unlucky unless it has come from someone with an incredibly happy marriage. The dress should never come from someone who has been prematurely widowed.

~ Never buy or borrow a wedding dress that was first bought or set aside for a wedding that never actually happened, as it is jinxed and you may be subjecting yourself to the same fate as the previous owner.

~ Never use a wedding dress that was first bought with the intention of marrying another fiancé.

~ Single female friends should sew some of their own hair into one of the hems or folds of the gown to bring about their own marriages within a short time.

~ The dress should not be completely finished before the actual wedding day. In some districts, it is customary for a short length of the hem to be left unsewn, so that a few stitches can be put in at the very last moment.

~ When the dress is being fitted, it should be put on in sections, never all at once.

~ The Bride when first trying on her wedding outfit, should put the clothes on over her feet, not over her head, for luck. *UK*

~ The Bride should always put her right arm into the right sleeve first. *German Pennsylvania: USA*

~ A Bride shouldn't try on her wedding dress before the wedding day or the wedding will not happen. *The Philippines*

~ It's good luck to put clothes on inside-out. If you accidentally put clothes on inside-out, you must not correct it that day, lest you take your good luck away. *Europe*

~ The Bride should not wear her entire outfit before the wedding day as it is unlucky for her to put on her full bridal array too soon. She should certainly never see herself completely dressed before the wedding service lest it jinx the marriage. Even on the Wedding Morning when she is checking her reflection, the Bride should leave off one part of the outfit, such as a glove.

~ When the Bride is admiring herself, she must be very careful not to offend the household spirits that dwell in the mirrors. *Eastern Europe*

~ The Bride must not let a female friend stand between her and mirror as the friend will steal her Groom. Likewise, the Groom should not let a male friend stand between *him* and the mirror when dressing. *Russia*

~ It's good luck for the fully dressed Bride to glance in her mirror just once before leaving for her wedding, but it is bad luck to look in the mirror after she has left the bedroom to commence her journey to the ceremony.

~ It's unlucky if the Groom sees his Bride wearing the wedding dress before the ceremony. *UK*

- If the Groom sees the Bride's dress before the day, his Bride will have bad luck during the ceremony. *Spain*

~ If clothes are left hanging out until sunset, she that puts them on will bewitch everybody. *Germany*

~ It is unlucky to wash anything on a Saturday.

~ It's lucky for the Bride to find a spider in her wedding gown.

~ If the Bride rips her wedding dress on the day, it means the marriage will soon end in death.

~ After the ceremony, the Bride should carefully remove all pins which were used in her wedding dress or veil, and give them to her friends or throw them away. If she keeps them or uses any of the pins in her going-away outfit, she will be very unlucky and the honeymoon will not be a happy one.

~ The Bride should not sell or loan out her dress after using it, as it's unlucky for her and tempting fate in her marriage.

The Dress's Colour

~ A white dress symbolises purity, innocence and simplicity.

~ Brides normally dressed in white to symbolise youth, joy and purity. *Ancient Greece & Rome*

~ A non-Virgin must never dress in a white dress as by wearing white she is claiming she is a virgin. If she does wear white, she will be lying to others and risking God's wrath. *Europe*

~ White is the colour of mourning, which is thought to be appropriate as the Bride is leaving her family of birth to join her husband's family, thereby undergoing a symbolic death with it. *China & Japan*

~ *'Married in white, you have chosen right.'* *UK & USA*

~ If a Bride marries in any colour other than white she will be poor. This belief probably came about because cloth was very expensive to bleach and more than one bleaching was required. The whiter the dress, the more affluent the Bride's family was. Also white dresses were extravagant as they couldn't be worn for any other occasion.

~ Grey, stone or fawn indicate a life of scrimping and saving: the reason being these colours were often chosen by simple Brides who preferred something that could be worn afterwards on Sundays and other special days.

~ *'Married in Pearl, you will live in a whirl.'* **UK & USA**

~ White, silver, blue, pink and gold are the luckiest colours of dress.

~ Yellow is widely disliked, since in country tradition it signifies 'foresworn.' **Rural UK**

~ *'Married in yellow, ashamed of your fellow.'* **UK & USA**

~ *'Married in blue, you (<u>or</u> your love) will always be true'* **UK & USA**

~ Blue has always been popular as it signifies constancy; *'Those dressed in blue have lovers true'.* **Northern UK**

~ Blue is the best colour for lovers.

~ Blue is unlucky: locals saying that *'if dressed in blue, she's sure to rue.'* **Yorkshire: UK**

~ Blue is so excellent a colour that 'something blue' must be worn for luck, even if the dress is of another colour.

~ Blue is the colour of the feminine; wearing blue thus embraces femininity, womanhood and fertility. **Navajo Tribe: USA**

~ Blue is the most sacred colour and is used to honour the tribal gods. **Hopi Tribe: USA**

~ Brides who marry in grey will travel far, as according to the rhyme;

'Married in Grey, you will go far away.' **UK & USA**

~ Nothing black should ever be worn by a Bride, as it is the colour of mourning and death.

~ *'Married in Black, you will wish yourself back.'* **UK & USA**

~ Fairies and other malicious wood spirits wear green, and anyone who wears green or otherwise favours the colour will come under the fairies' evil influence. **UK**

~ It's unlucky for a Bride to wear green as the fairies might steal her away. **Ireland**

~ Green was once thought so ill-omened for *any occasion* that not only the Bride but the wedding guests were forbidden from wearing it. The reason being was that the fairies, whose chosen colour it was, would resent the insult and destroy the wearer. **Scottish Lowlands** [6]

~ Green foretells a change into mourning clothes whenever it is worn as 'Anyone who wears green will have to wear black soon afterwards'. It should never ever be considered for weddings. **UK**

~ The old expression that a woman has a 'green gown' was used to imply promiscuity, the green staining being due to rolling about in grassy fields with their lovers.

~ *'Married in green, ashamed to be seen.'* **UK & USA**

~ *'Green and white, forsaken quite.'* **Rural Northern UK**

~ A green dress is always unlucky unless the Bride is Irish. **Ireland**

~ Brown is to be avoided as those who are married in it, *'will never live in a town.'* This means that their husbands will never rise in life or acquire riches. Some traditional rhymes, however, say the opposite; 'Married in Brown, you *will* live in town.' **UK & USA**

~ A red wedding dress symbolises love and joy. **China**

~ A red dress indicates a brazen and 'scarlet woman'. *UK*

~ *'Married in red, you will wish yourself dead.'* *UK & USA*

~ Red drives off evil as blood and anything that looks like blood has the power to drive away evil. Emperor Albinus's family (196 A.D) had their newborns wrapped in bandages of a reddish colour for this reason. *Ancient Rome* [16]

~ The Bride should dress in red, or at the least put a red ribbon in her hair, or somewhere on her person (e.g. around the wrist) to protect herself from spells and curses and the 'Evil Eye'. *Gypsy, Jewish, Europe, Belize etc.*

~ *'Married in pink, of you he'll think.'* *USA*

~ *'Married in pink, your spirit will sink'* (some rhymes say *'stink'*). *UK*

~ Purple is a mourning colour so should not be worn for weddings.

~ Purple was worn as a protective garment against spirits and spells. *Ancient Rome*

~ Some may choose their colour of outfit according to the Day they marry on. Monday's astrological colour is White, Tuesday's colour is Red, Wednesday's colour is Purple, Thursday's colour is Blue, Friday's Colour is Green, Saturday's Colour is Black, and Sunday's colour is Yellow.

The Wedding Veil

~ In ancient times, the veil was a complete head to toe covering, worn to confuse evil spirits from knowing who exactly was getting married.

~ Brides wore red or yellow veils representing fire to ward off demons that may attack the Bride and her fertility. *Ancient Greece & Rome*

~ The Mother of the Bride places the veil on the Bride before the wedding ceremony to symbolise the last task a Mother does on behalf of her daughter before she becomes a married woman. *Poland*

~ An old bridal veil is luckier than a new one, particularly if it is a family heirloom or is borrowed from a happily married woman. The good fortune and fertility of the earlier marriage passes with the veil onto its new wearer.

~ If the Bride does not wear a veil or some kind of head covering, she is not submitting herself to God or to her husband, and will therefore make an unruly wife within an unhappy and unblessed marriage.

~ White storks, pomegranates, fish, fowl, wheat and midwives were all popular illustrations on bridal veils, expressing the couple's wish for children. *Jewish* [13]

~ Finding a tear in the wedding veil is an omen of good luck.

~ The veil should never be put on before the wedding morning except during essential fittings, and then it must be tried on separately, not with the dress.

~ It is unlucky to wear or see oneself in the veil too soon. If a Bride looks at herself in the mirror while wearing the veil on any other occasion than her wedding day, her marriage will be unhappy, or may not even come about.

~ When she is dressing for the ceremony on the big day, the veil should not be put on until the Bride is completely ready, nor should she see herself in it until she takes one last look at herself in the mirror before heading for the church.

~ Dropping the veil during the ceremony spells unhappiness for the couple. *The Philippines*

Wedding Shoes *(See also pages 47 & 91)*

~ If the Groom buckles his Bride's left shoe on the wedding day, she'll have the mastery within the marriage. ***Germany***[3]

~ If one of the Brides' heels from her wedding shoes snaps, her family life will be lame. ***Russia***

~ If a woman tears her wedding shoes, she'll be beaten by her husband. ***Germany***[3]

~ Names of single girls (usually the Bridesmaids) are written on the undersole of one of the Bride's shoes; the name that remains written there after the ceremony will marry soon. ***Turkey***

~ When the Bride is about to go to church, all her old shoes are hidden away and new shoes are given to her by the Groom. In Roussillon, it is always the nearest relative to the Groom who puts on the Bride's new shoes for her. The meaning of this custom comes out clearer in Berry, where all the assistants try to put the Bride's shoes on, but fail, and only the Groom succeeds...echoing the tale of Cinderella. This superstition relates to the mythology of shoes (Chapter 8). ***France & Germany***

Underwear

~ When dressing for the ceremony, be sure to put on the right stocking and the right shoe first for luck. ***German Pennsylvania***

~ If the Groom ties the Bride's garters for her, she'll give birth with easy labours each time. ***Germany***[3]

~ The Bride must give one of her stockings to a Bridesmaid, who will then throw it onto the wedding guests. On whomever the stocking lands, he or she will be the next to marry. ***Germany***[3]

~ If the Bride loses her garter in the street, her husband will become unfaithful to her.

~ At the end of the wedding celebration, the Bride and Groom are to sit down on the marriage bed, fully dressed except for their shoes and socks/stockings. One of the Bridesmaids takes off the Groom's sock, sits down on the floor with her back against the bed and throws it with her left hand over her right shoulder, aiming for the face of the Groom. All the Bridesmaids then repeat this, and the one who succeeds will soon marry. The Bride's stocking is then removed by the young men and thrown in the same fashion, thereby determining which of them will marry next. *Germany*[3]

~ The Groom must remove the Bride's garter and throw it back over his shoulder towards the unmarried male guests. The one who catches it will be the next to marry.

~ The man who catches the garter should place it on the leg of the girl who caught the bouquet. The recipients of the bouquet and garter should have a photograph taken with the Bride and Groom for luck. *USA*

~ After the ceremony, young men raced from the church porch to the Bride's home. The winner was then allowed to remove the garter from the Bride's leg which he placed on his own sweetheart's leg as a love charm against unfaithfulness. *Pickering: Yorkshire*

~ After the wedding, the Bride should hide her girdle in the threshold of the house, so that the Groom will step over it and bring eternal luck and desire to the marriage. *Germany*[3]

~ Brides pinned a small pouch to their petticoat. Inside the pouch they put a small piece of bread, some cloth, a piece of wood, and a one-dollar bill. By doing this, the newlyweds would always be assured of enough food, clothes, shelter, and money. *USA*

~ A Red ribbon attached to the petticoat or garter wards off evil spirits *(see page 57)*. *Jewish & European* Blue ribbons ward off witchcraft and the evil eye. *UK*

~ To overcome Bad Omens, evil spirits and witchcraft, the Bride should carry salt somewhere on her person. This is often secreted somewhere in her undergarments or hems.

~ A 'Magic Handkerchief' brings luck and fertility. This special hanky with a few stitches can be turned into a special christening bonnet for the couple's first baby. *Ireland*

Jewellery

~ Wear earrings for the ceremony and you will always be happy.

~ A happily-married female friend should put on the Bride's earrings for her, so the Bride will have a happy marriage. *Russia*

~ A Bride who wears pearls on her wedding will be an unhappy wife experiencing much heartache and tears. *The Philippines & Mexico*

~ If any jewellery falls off at the wedding, it's a bad omen. *Russia*

~ Cowrie shells are traditionally worn in a Bride's necklace, and used to trim her wedding dress and headpiece in silver and white to encourage her fertility. The shell is also a symbol of beauty and power. *Africa*

~ The Bride must wear a cross or crucifix for luck and God's blessing on her big day. *Europe*

~ The faith, hope and charity charm is a fitting charm for the Wedding Day.

~ All metal (particularly iron) wards off evil spirits.

~ Only pure metals should be worn: alloys are bad luck.

~ Silver is associated with the Moon, a symbol of the goddess, the feminine and fertility.

~ Bridal ornaments for the head and neck often represent the moon's phase in its first quarter for fertility reasons. *Sweden* [4]

~ Brides wore golden crowns. After the wedding, unmarried women danced in a circle around the blindfolded Bride, while the Bride attempted to place the crown on one of the girl's heads. She who got the crown would marry first. *Finland*

~ If the crown falls of the Bride or Groom during the ceremony one of them will soon be widowed. *Russia*

~ Silver jewellery, or a gold and silver crown from which silver decorations dangled were worn by the Bride. During the 'The Dance Off' at the reception later, the silver tinkled loudly, its sound frightening off any evil spirits. *Norway*

~ The jingling of iron and the tinkling of the bells on iron anklets prevents demons from entering. *Africa Slave Coast*

~ A black bracelet, talisman or image of Buddha ensures the Bride's well-being. *China*

~ An Owl's eye worn on a string around the neck is an effective talisman against being 'overlooked' with the Evil Eye. *Morocco*

~ To protect against being 'overlooked' tie a black thread around the wrist or to the gold bangles worn on the arm. *India & Bangladesh*

Something Old

~ The 'something old' represents the couple's friends and family. Wearing 'something old' expresses the wish that they will stay close during the marriage.

~ The 'something old' must come from a happily married female, lest the item bring ill-luck to the marriage.

Something New

~ 'Something new' symbolises the newlyweds' happy and prosperous future.

~ Because she is entering a new state of life, every item of the Bride's clothing should be completely new. Even pins that have been used before should be rejected. The only exception to this rule is the 'wearing of something old' and 'something borrowed.' *Shropshire: UK*

Something Borrowed

~ 'Something borrowed' should not come from a widow, lest the Bride soon become a widow herself. Neither should it come from a bitter divorcee for obvious reasons! 'Something borrowed' should be from an older woman in the family who has a happy marriage. The Bride must return the borrowed item to ensure the good luck stays with her.

~ The loan of a wedding dress means good luck to the borrower and bad luck for the lender.

Something Blue

~ The custom of the Bride wearing 'something blue' originated in ancient Israel where the Bride wore a blue ribbon in her hair to represent fidelity.

~ Blue symbolises constancy, loyalty, faithfulness, and good luck.

~ Blue is the symbol of eternity, heaven and spirituality.

~ The Bride should wear or carry something blue to increase her luck.

~ *'Touch blue and your wish will come true.'* **UK**

~ A Bride should wear an old blue apron underneath her wedding dress for luck. **Germany** [3]

~ Wearing blue protects from witches. Even a little blue on the underside of the Bride's shoes is enough to ward off their evil power.

~ Tiny blue eye medallions deflect the Evil Eye. **Greece & Turkey**

And a silver sixpence in your shoe

~ Coins were put in the Bride's shoe to placate Diana, the Goddess of Chastity, so the Bride could lose her virginity and conceive a child. **Ancient Greece**

~ Placing a silver sixpence in the Bride's left shoe brings the Bride both financial *and* emotional wealth. In some areas, it was believed that the Father of the Bride should place the sixpence in his daughter's shoe.

~ If the Bride and Groom place a three-headed bohemian coin under the sole of their right foot on the wedding day, theirs will be a happy marriage. **Germany** [3]

~ The Bride *and* the Groom should have coins placed underneath *both* of their heels. **Russia**

Other

~ It's a bad omen if the Bride loses a glove before the big day. **Russia**

~ To be sure of a 'sweet life', a Bride should carry a lump of sugar in her glove on wedding day. **Greece**

~ If a Bride wishes to rule her husband, let her on the wedding day dress in a baking trough. **Germany** [3]

~ Brides must change their outfits several times throughout their wedding day for luck. *Japan*

~ Changing out of your wedding clothes before nightfall brings bad luck.

~ In the Highlands of Perthshire down to the end of the eighteenth century, every knot was carefully unloosed in the clothes of the Bride and Groom before the ceremony so any spell preventing consummation of the marriage would be rendered invalid. *Scotland* [14]

~ Brides should carry a horseshoe for good luck and fertility (turned prongs upwards so the luck won't run out). *Ireland*

~ The reason for the horseshoe's magical power is because the horse and the ass were in the stable where Christ was born, and so became blessed animals. *Ireland* [4]

~ The froth from a horse's mouth repels demons, who fear horses more than any other animal. The horseshoe represents this repellent power. *Hindustan* [4]

~ Put pins in the Bride and Groom's clothes to ward off the malignancy of the 'evil eye'. *Russia*

~ The Bride wears a special amulet against evil familiar spirits consisting of an inch long triangular bag of coloured cloth. This bag contains seeds and is fastened to her hair at the back. *Egypt* [15]

~ A Bride secretes on her person portions of Holy Scripture to protect her from evil spirits. Or she wears an amulet containing or inscribed with a verse with talismanic power. *Jewish & Islamic*

~ The Bride should put some of her clothing on inside-out and tuck a piece of garlic and bread inside her clothing to protect her from the 'evil eye'. *Russia*

~ A piece of bread and cheese were placed in the Bride's clothing to guard against fairy abduction en-route to the Church. *Ireland*

~ The 'going away' outfit should be as simple as possible, lest bad luck be brought upon the happy pair.

The Groom's Outfit

~ The Groom should not wear black, the colour of mourning. The luckiest colour for a wedding suit is grey.

~ On his wedding day, a man should wear a shirt has Bride given him for luck.

~ The Groom should be married in a blue bathing apron. *Germany* [3]

~ After a hair trim, the Groom's family and close male friends rub turmeric paste on his face and over his chest. Turmeric leaves the skin with a golden glow and is supposed to bring luck and ward off evil spirits. *East India*

~ As a protection against magic, the Groom steps three times over a bundle of his old clothes containing some of his shaved-off hair. *Morocco* [14]

~ The people who help a Groom dress ensure that no knot is tied or no button buttoned, as this would give power to the Groom's enemies to magically deprive him of his conjugal rights. *Syria* [15]

~ The Groom should put on his clothes over his feet, not over his head for luck. *UK*

~ The Groom should dress putting on his right shoe and sock first and put his right arm into his right sleeve first. *German Pennsylvania*

~ It is lucky to wear a pair of socks with a small hole in them. *UK*

~ The Groom should spit on his shoes for luck when polishing them.

~ The 'horn of plenty' charm brings potency and virility as well as plenty to the marriage. *Italy*

~ The Groom should carry a tiny horseshoe charm for luck.

~ Insert money, bread, and garlic somewhere into the Groom's outfit; then the first two will never fail him, and the garlic will protect him from sorcery.

~ If the Groom's friend cuts a piece off the Groom's tie, he'll get married himself soon. *Spain*

CHAPTER 4

WEDDING FLOWERS

~ Wedding bouquets were originally made of strong smelling herbs and spices such as thyme and garlic to frighten away evil spirits that would seek to ruin the marriage. *Ancient Greece*

~ Bridal bouquets were a mixture of flowers and herbs. The flowers were symbolic amongst other things of fertility, and the strong smelling herbs repelled evil. *Medieval Europe*

~ Two little flower girls scattered yellow rose petals flowers before the Bride, so the marriage would be fertile. *UK*

~ To promote their fertility, Brides carried bunches of herbs under their wedding veils and both Bride and Groom wore floral garlands symbolising the hope for new life. *Ancient Rome*

~ Mistletoe is an ancient fertility charm in many different cultures, and was widely used in Bride's floral garlands. *Switzerland*

~ Orange Blossoms represent fertility and were often used at weddings for this reason. Juno, Goddess of maternity and childbirth, was said to have given Orange Blossoms to Jupiter on her wedding day. *Ancient Rome*

~ Carrying a bouquet of flowers signifies a woman in bloom.

~ If it rains on the bridal wreath, the couple will be rich and fertile. *Germany* [1]

~ A combination of just red and white flowers should be avoided because red and white stands for 'blood and bandages'. *UK*

~ Putting lavender into the Bride's bouquet brings good fortune and makes all her wishes come true. *Ireland*

51

~ The Bride & Groom strolling down a pathway decorated with evergreen represents constancy. *Germany*

~ All green flowers and floral greenery should be avoided or you will offend the fairies, whose colour it is. *Scottish Lowlands*

~ As a wish for wisdom, love and loyalty for the Bride, her friends weave her a rosemary wreath on the night before the wedding to carry at the ceremony. *Rural Czech Republic*

~ The bouquet was adorned with several ribbons and knots. There had to be at least three knots for good luck, and the ribbons were tied with a 'lover's knot', the symbol of eternity. *Victorian UK*

~ Brides traditionally carry live myrtle (symbolising love), and then give cuttings to their Bridesmaids. If, when the Bridesmaid plants the myrtle, it roots and blossoms, she will marry within a year. *Wales*

~ Clover protects from witch's spells and fairies, and brings good luck.

~ Angelica and nettle worn as an amulet will protect from evil spirits.

~ The wedding flowers were very carefully selected for the idea or emotion that they symbolized within the 'language of flowers' (see the next page). *Victorian UK*

~ In ancient times, it was believed that a Bride was especially lucky on her wedding day. Guests would sometimes tear at her dress for a piece of good luck to take home with them. The tossing of the bridal bouquet came into being as a replacement good luck souvenir that prevented guests from bothering the Bride and her dress.

~ It is good luck for the Bride to throw her wedding bouquet backwards over her shoulder towards the guests when she leaves for her honeymoon. The one who catches it will be the next to be married.

~ The bridesmaid to first get a sprig of the bouquet will marry next.

The Language of Flowers

NB: The meanings can vary from place to place. I have included the most commonly accepted meanings.

Red Chrysanthemum: means 'I love you.'

Apple Blossom: Better things to come, preference

Agapanthus: Love letters

Anemone: Farewell to the past

Antherinium: No secrets from you

Asparagus Fern: Sincerity

Azaleas: Temperance

Birch: Longevity

Camelia: Gratitude

Carnation: Pure love and fascination or unhappiness in love.

Chrysanthemum: Wealth and truth

White Chrysanthemum: Cheerfulness and truth

Cornflower: Admiration and hope

Cotton Balls: Nature

Cyclamen: Shyness and modesty

Daffodil: Regard

Daisy: Innocence

White Daisy: Beauty and innocence

Delphinium: An open heart

Fern: Fascination and sincerity

Flowering Almond: Hope

Forget-me not: Remembrance and true love

Freesia: Innocence and trust

Geranium: Thoughts of youth

Gerbera: Loyal love

Gypsophila: Innocence

Heliotrope: Faithfulness and Devotion

Hollyhock: Devotion

Honeysuckle: The Bond of Love, Generosity

Hyacinth: Loveliness

Hydrangea: Boastfulness

Iris: Faith and wisdom

Ivy: Eternal fidelity

Ivy Leaves: The lasting bond of marriage

Japonica: Loveliness

Jasmine: Amiability

Lavender: Sweetness Joy

Lemon Blossom: Fidelity in love

Lilac: Youthful Innocence, humility and purity

Lily: Majesty, Beauty & Honour (NB: lilies are thought unlucky by many because of their association with death)

Lily of the Valley: Happiness renewed, return of happiness: (the choice of flower for many widows who remarry)

Magnolia: Love of nature, nobility, perseverance

Maidenhead fern: Discretion

Mimosa: Sensitivity

Miniature Rose: Remember always

Moss: Affection always

Myrtle: Constancy in affection and duty

Narcissus: Stay sweet forever

Orange Blossom: Eternal love, purity, chastity, loveliness, fertility – have been associated with weddings since ancient times.

Orchid: Refinement, love

Pansy: 'Think of me'

Peach Blossom: Captive

Peony: Captivation (peonies are avoided by some as they can represent shame)

Poppy: Pleasure

Protea: Enchantment, magic

Rhododendron: Fascination

Red Rose: True Love, respect, courage

Deep Red Rose: Beauty & passion

Pale Pink Rose: Grace, Joy & Happiness

Dark Pink Rose: Thankfulness, friendship, admiration

Coral Rose: Passion and desire

Peach Rose: Modesty and purity, gratitude, admiration, sympathy

Yellow Rose: Friendship, joy, jealousy, freedom, hope

Orange Rose: Fascination

Lavender Rose: Enchantment, uniqueness

White Rose: Innocence, Pure spiritual and eternal love, humility

Tea Roses: 'I'll remember always'

Red & White Roses: Unity, Engagement, or 'blood and bandages'

Yellow & Orange Roses: Passionate thoughts

Yellow & Red Roses: Congratulations

Rosebuds: Youth and beauty, a heart innocent of love

Red Rosebuds: Purity and loveliness

White Rosebuds: A young innocent love, girlhood

Rosemary: Remembrance

Snapdragon: Graciousness

Snowdrop: Hope

Spray Carnation: Fascination

Stargazer Lily: Wealth, Stock, Affectionate bonds

Sunflower: Splendid beauty

Sweet Pea: Delicate pleasure

Tulip: My perfect lover, declaration of love

Twisted Willow: Remembrance

Verbena Lemon: Freshness of spirit

Veronica: Fidelity

Violet: Faithfulness, innocence; lucky for lovers

Blue Violet: Love

CHAPTER 5

'THE GUEST LIST'

Beware Of The Evil Eye

~ The belief in the power of the 'Evil Eye' is an ancient belief that has spread far and wide. When someone looks at you or something close to your heart with envy they may intentionally or not put a hex on you and your family resulting in sickness, injury, poverty, or death.

At certain times such as marriage, one is said to be particularly vulnerable to The Evil Eye's influence. Therefore, the engaged couple must be very careful not to invite anyone with the Evil Eye to their wedding, and/or take all possible precautions just in case someone slips through the net inadvertently.

~ If someone looks enviously at a healthy Bride they can 'overlook' her, cursing her marriage and making her wither.

~ Those who have the 'evil eye' may not be aware they have it or are doing anything bad. Hairy people, deformed people, and those with a squint or eyebrows that meet in the middle are often thought to be possessors of the evil eye, as also are blue-eyed people in Mediterranean countries.

~ A woman on her period is prone to giving the Evil Eye. *Guyana*

~ To ward off the evil eye, make the 'mano cornuto' horn sign. This entails making the hand into a fist and extending the index and little finger. This hand gesture has its origins as an ancient amulet. *Italy*

~ Alternatively, douse the Bride & Groom in coconut oil. *Trinidad*

~ The word 'Garlic' protects from the evil eye. If anyone utters a word of praise with intent of bewitching or of doing harm, cry aloud

'Garlic!' or utter it three times rapidly. ***Poland, Greece & Turkey*** [18]

~ Carry a black marble for protection from the 'evil eye' at night, and a white marble for protection during the day. ***Bedouin Tribes***

~ Placate the suspected possessor of the evil eye with beer and tobacco. ***Africa***

~ The evil eye has to be countered by chanting, 'Whoever gave you the evil eye may it fall on them' three times in Yiddish. ***Jewish***

~ Passages from the Koran are painted as murals on the walls to ward off the evil eye. ***Islamic***

Other Dangers

~ Bonfires and other light sources drive away malevolent spirits. ***UK***

~ Swallow fresh butter to protect yourself from the fairies. ***Scotland***

~ An open Bible should be placed somewhere in the room where the wedding reception is to be held for protection. ***Italy***

~ No evil spirit enters a room where a Holy Book is given the place of honour on the highest shelf. ***Islamic***

Bridesmaids

~ Ushers and Bridesmaids were dressed like the Bride and Groom, acting as decoys so that the Devil and his evil spirits would not know who was getting married.

~ Red hair indicates good luck, and is called bálá kámeskro, or sun hairs. It is therefore very lucky to have a red-headed bridesmaid or Best Man. ***Romany Gypsy*** [18]

~ Redheads will be fiery-tempered *(UK & USA)*, are unlucky, especially at New Year *(UK)*, are to be feared *(Holland)* and are untrustworthy so should never be asked to be Bridesmaids.

~ Redheads are the devil's own (Judas Iscariot was said to have had red hair).

~ Redheads are held to be evil, malicious and unlucky, probably because Typhon, the evil principle, was red; therefore a red heifer was sacrificed to him by the Egyptians. *Ireland*[2]

~ Redheads are always born of an illicit affair, or as some say, are "the milkman's". They therefore have low morals and will try to seduce the Groom. *UK*

~ Yellow hair was likewise regarded in years gone by with ill favour and almost viewed a deformity. *UK*[10]

~ Children with curls might be fairies in disguise. Golden curls suggest mermaids, whereas elves are chocolate curled. Red curls are indicative of a witch, and raven curls indicate a very powerful fairy indeed. *Scotland*[10]

~ The plainer the Bridesmaid, the luckier the Bride!

~ *'Twice a Bridesmaid, never a Bride.'* In some places, it is three times.

~ Should a Bridesmaid be older than the Bride she must wear something green, or she will never succeed in finding a husband.

The Best Man

~ Do not ask someone to be a Best Man if their eyebrows meet in the middle, as it indicates a jealous, bad-tempered disposition. *UK*

~ The Best Man must arrange for the Groom to carry a small mascot or charm in his pocket on the wedding day.

~ The Best Man must ensure that once the Groom has began his journey to the church he does not return for any reason as that is very unlucky.

~ When the Best Man pays the Church minister's fee, he should pay an odd sum to bring the couple luck.

Wedding Guests

~ Roman law required ten witnesses to outwit the evil spirits attending happy events. ***Ancient Rome***

~ Never be a witness at more than two weddings or you'll end up single. ***Russia***

~ Never have an odd number of guests at your wedding.

~ A total of 13 people at a wedding is incredibly unlucky.

~ Twins are unlucky and are to be feared. ***Africa***

~ A widow or barren woman should not be invited to the wedding, as her bad luck may rub off on the Bride. ***India***

~ A pregnant woman's presence brings bad luck. ***Vietnam***

~ A menstruating guest is unlucky and may jinx the Bride. ***Belize***

~ If a child cries during the service, it's a lucky sign.

~ A baby boy, placed in the Bride's lap, blesses her with sons. ***Turkey***

~ The Bride should kiss a baby's head at her wedding to bring her swift conception.

~ Having the family cat or dog at a wedding grants luck and fertility to the newlyweds.

~ When dogs fight at a wedding, it is an omen that the happy pair will come to blows. ***Germany*** [3]

~ As the Bride is lucky, she should pray under her wedding canopy for an infertile woman's fertility. ***Jewish***

~ It's fatal to tie a knot in a red handkerchief at a marriage, and only an enemy does it. To break the spell, the kerchief must be burned. [2]

CHAPTER 6

THE WEDDING DAY

Preparing The Ceremony Place

~ A marriage taking place anywhere else but Church is tempting fate. In many people's eyes, such a marriage is not a 'real' marriage anyway.

~ A woman must not be married in the same church that she was christened in.

~ Ribbons are used to decorate the room and to signify the tying of two lives together.

~ Mirrors are dwelling places of spirits so should not be placed in the ceremony area. However, if there is already a mirror there do not cover it up lest you offend the spirit dwelling there. *Russia*

~ It's bad luck to have visible mirrors within the Ceremony area.

~ Hanging up mirrors near the entrance will guard against the fairies as although fairies love to look at their reflections in pools of water, they hate mirrors. *Ireland*

~ Mirrors are placed on front doors. If a dragon tries to get in, he'll see his reflection, think there is already a dragon there, and go away. *Vietnam*

~ A Mirror of any size placed opposite the door will reflect back out of the door any evil or spell that comes in.

~ Candles in the Church ward off evil spirits. *Medieval Europe*

~ If candles lit on a wedding day sputter out, an evil spirit is nearby.

~ A flame extinguished on one of the wedding candles means the partner on whose side the unlit candle was, will die ahead of the other. *The Philippines*

~ Candles are used to represent new beginnings and the joining together of two families. ***USA***

~ Candles carved with certain key words can raise magical power. ***Wiccan***

The Wedding Morning

~ A Bride who awakes to the sound of singing birds on her wedding day is very lucky as it means that she and her husband will never quarrel, and will remain true to one another forever.

~ It is lucky to hear a cuckoo on the wedding morning, or to see three magpies. ***Ireland***

~ It is unlucky to hear a rooster crow after the break of dawn on one's wedding day.

~ If a bird crows on the day, the Bride will cry before St. Patrick's Day (March 17th) ***Isle of Man*** [16]

~ If a cat sneezes near the Bride on the morning of the wedding, she will have a happy life.

~ It is unlucky for the Bride and Groom to see each other before the ceremony.

~ On the wedding day, man and wife must wash crosswise so they can't be bewitched. ***Germany*** [3]

~ A Bride's wedding day tears are good luck as they bring rain for crops and new growth.

~ Bridal tears during the ceremony are considered lucky, but tears at any other moment during the day predict a marriage full of tears.

~ If the Bride sheds a tear on her wedding day, she will never cry again for the duration of her marriage. ***Victorian UK***

~ A laughing Bride becomes a weeping wife.

~ If the Groom smiles a lot, his first child will be a daughter. **Korea**

~ If Bride or Groom have an injury on them on their wedding day, they'll carry it to the grave with them, as it will never heal. **Germany**[3]

The Weather on the Big Day

~ The Bride will have fair weather if she feeds the cat well just before leaving for the church.

~ It will rain at her wedding if an unmarried girl eats the brown that sticks inside the porridge pot **Germany** [3] or if she eats anything directly from the pot. **Brazil**

~ To ensure it won't rain and to bring good luck, a statue of the Infant of Prague should be put outside the church. **Ireland**

~ It is lucky if the sun shines on the Bride. '*Happy is the Bride that the sun shines on; But blessed is the corpse that the rain rains on.*' **Ireland**[2]

~ It's lucky if the Bride sees a rainbow on her Wedding Day.

~ Fair or foul weather upon the wedding day indicates a happy or unhappy married life. **New Orleans: USA**[7]

~ A windy day predicts a turbulent marriage.

~ If it rains, the new couple will become rich. **Russia**

~ Rain on your wedding day means you will have many children. **Italy**

~ If it rains on the bridal wreath, the couple will be rich and fertile. **Germany** [3]

~ Rain during the wedding means prosperity and happiness for the newlyweds. **Philippines**

~ Rain on your wedding day is lucky as 'a wet knot is harder to untie'. **UK**

~ If it rains when a Bride is on her way to church, she has been crying; if the sun shines, she has been laughing. *Germany* [3]

~ Rain on the wedding day means frequent weeping for the wife. *Estonia* [3]

~ A wet day is very unlucky, as the Bride will weep for sorrow throughout the year. *Ireland* [2]

~ If it rains while a wedding party are on their way to the church, or returning from it, it indicates a life of marital bickering and unhappiness. *Cornwall* [17]

~ A rainy day foretells a sad, wretched marriage. *Germany* [3] *& Spain*

~ Snow on the wedding day is associated with fertility and wealth.

~ Snow on the wedding day foretells a happy marriage. *Germany* [3]

~ Snow is considered a greater blessing than rain. *Native American*

~ '*Bride's day white, every ditch full of black or of white.*'

Leaving the House for the Ceremony

~ Salt was carried around the Bride 'withershins' (backwards) to protect her from evil during the sometimes long journey to the church where the ceremony was to be performed. *Scotland*

~ The Bride must leave her home by the front door, and must step over the threshold with her right foot leading.

~ Bride and Groom, on your way to church avoid the house-eaves, and do not look around. *Germany* [3]

~ It's the custom to pour a kettleful of boiling water over the doorstep just after the Bride has left her old home; as before it dries up another marriage is sure to be agreed on. *Yorkshire: UK* [6]

~ The doorstep was well scrubbed with soap and water directly after the Bride left the house; to wash away the impress of her foot and to show that the old home was no longer a home to her, as she had chosen another. *Devon: UK* [6]

~ When the Bride leaves the house, the floor is washed so she will not return there. *Russia*

~ As the Bride goes to church, throw the keys after her, so she'll be economical. *Germany* [3]

Wedding Transport

~ It's very lucky for the Bride to travel in a carriage drawn by a grey horse. It's unlucky if the horses gallop to the wedding though. *Europe*

~ In the wedding ride the driver may not turn the horses, nor rein them in; else the marriage will be childless. *Germany* [3]

~ When the Bride is set down at the church door, the coachman must drive on for some way before turning, since to turn the horses' heads immediately outside the building brings bad luck.

~ A wedding car should never be black as that is the colour of a hearse and mourning. *UK & USA*

~ Decorating the wedding car with red ribbons represents virginity; blue ribbons depict the opposite. *Russia*

~ Flowers decorate the front of the wedding car so the Bride and Groom will have happy travels throughout their life together. *Italy*

~ A Bride has power over the sea on her wedding day: if she steers a boat, the wind and wave will not be able to damage it, however strong the storm. *Ireland* [2]

~ It's a bad sign if the car or horses are reluctant to start or break down, either on the way to or from the church.

En-route to The Ceremony

~ The Bride, Groom, Best Man, and Maid of Honour formed a mini-procession to walk to church. The Bride would go first, with the Best Man, Groom, and Maid of Honour following behind. On the return trip, Bride and Groom would walk in front, with the Best Man and Maid of Honour walking as a pair behind them.

~ Young girls carried wheat before the Bride in the marriage procession, symbolising the wish the marriage would be fertile. *UK*

~ A Bride that means to have the mastery in the marriage shall dawdle, and let the Groom get to church before her. *Germany*[3]

~ In walking to your wedding, don't look around you. *Germany*[3]

~ To ensure good luck, the Groom should give a coin or a gift of food to the first person the party encounter. On the way back from the church, this duty falls to the Bride.

~ To be first met by a gypsy is a very fortunate omen indeed.

> *'When you are going along the street*
> *It's lucky a gypsy man to meet.'*[18]

~ In the UK it is extremely lucky to be met by a chimney sweep on your wedding day. Although the original reason for this superstition has been lost, I believe it may be to do with the ancient belief in the protecting power of fire and light. Evil spirits and wicked fairies were believed to depart the house via the chimney and the household hearth was thought to placate spirits or keep them at bay. Furthermore, in India, soot from the fire is believed to ward off all evil spirits.

~ It's **lucky** to see: black cats, spiders, toads, lambs, elephants, a woman carrying a jug full of water, and grey horses.

~ It's **unlucky** to see on the way to the Church: pigs, hares, cats, dogs, lizards, serpents, owls, a funeral procession, a woman carrying an *empty* jug of water, police officers, doctors, lawyers, the blind, a cartload of dung and pregnant women.

~ Meeting a nun or a monk foretells barrenness.

~ It's unlucky in all Catholic countries to meet a priest or nun, especially when he or she is the first person encountered in the morning, probably because of the belief that any person connected with celibacy and chastity is unlucky. [18]

~ According to a widely spread and ancient belief, it's very lucky to meet with any woman of easy virtue - the easier the better. This is doubtless derived from the ancient worship of Venus. [18]

~ If a stone rolls towards a wedding pair walking to church, it is an evil omen. ***Germany*** [3]

~ Crossing running water is unlucky. One of the wedding party must transfer the ill luck by finding a small object, then cursing it instead by saying 'Bad luck cleave to you,' and throwing it into the water.

~ No bridal procession ever passed over Gold Bridge on its way to or from the church. To do so would be extremely unlucky. The reason for this strongly held belief was that, according to a local legend, St. Edmund, King and Martyr, hid under this bridge when he fled from the victorious Danes in A.D. 870. A newly-married couple, passing that way by moonlight, saw the reflection of his gift spurs in the water, and betrayed him to the Danes, who then murdered him. As a punishment for their treachery, the King laid a powerful curse upon every bridal pair who crossed the bridge in the future on their way to or from their wedding. ***Suffolk: UK*** [6]

~ If there is a grave open during a wedding, it is unlucky. The bad luck depends on whether the grave is for a man, woman or child; in the first case the Bride will be a widow, in the second, the Groom a widower, in the last case, the couple's children will all die early. *Germany*[3]

~ Carrying an open red umbrella over the bride protects her from evil spirits. *China*

~ If the Bride falls on her way to Church, it foretells the early death of her first three or four children. *Estonia*[3]

~ If the Groom stumbles, he's not sure. *Russia*

~ If the people of their parish approved of the marriage, they threw rice, pots, pans, brushes and other household items at the couple as they approached the church. *Ireland*

~ Bridal parties must *never* enter the church through the Lych-gate; as this gate is reserved for funerals and will bring bad luck.

~ The Bride 'walks with the sun' to her wedding (east to west on the south side of the church) to ensure her fertility, since the sun and fertility are associated. She then circles the Church three times 'sunwise' for luck. *Scotland*

~ Wedding parties should always enter Church by its South or West Doors. Passing through the North Door of the Church brings bad luck as in many parishes it was reserved solely for funerals.

~ Demons come from the North where the Norse (Pagan) gods live; therefore the North Door of the Church must not be entered for a wedding. *Medieval UK*

~ A ribbon is tied across the front of the church door to represent the bond of marriage. *Italy*

~ Salt and or pepper may be scattered at the Church Door to dispel evil. *Medieval Europe*

~ A bench or stool is placed at the church door, over which the Bride and Groom must leap to symbolise they are entering a new life state. *UK* [6]

Entering the Ceremony Area

~ The Groom must arrive before the Bride to avoid bad luck. *The Philippines*

~ The sound of the church bells ringing as the Bride and Groom enter and leave the church drives away evil spirits, thereby ensuring the couple good fortune and fertility.

~ The Groom should spit or blow his nose three times before entering the Church for luck. *Europe*

~ Spittle is 'soul-stuff' and is lucky, often used for healing and warding off evil spirits. Therefore several of the wedding party may spit for luck. *Islamic*

~ If a Bride wishes to rule her husband, she should knock at the church door. *Germany* [3]

~ The Bride should step with her right foot first into the church to ensure good luck.

Up the Aisle To The Altar

~ Rose petals are thrown before the Bride as she walks down the aisle to ward off the evil spirits coming up at her from beneath the ground and to grant her fertility.

~ When the Bride is fetched in, she must wear no chains or bells, but be led in solemn silence; or she'll have restless noisy children. *Estonia* [3]

~ It's bad luck for the Bride to start down the aisle on time.

~ The Bride should step on the Groom's foot while walking towards the altar if she wants him to agree to her every whim.

The Philippines

~ At a wedding, the Bride should tread on the Groom's foot, so that she may never be oppressed by him. *Estonia*[3]

~ A large hawthorn tree that stood in the middle of a field near a stream was hung all over with bits of coloured stuff, while lighted rush candles were placed amongst its branches, to symbolise the new life of brightness for the bridal pair.

A boy carried a lighted torch of bogwood representing Hymen: the flame of love being his cognizance. After him came the betrothed pair hand-in-hand, a large square canopy of black stuff being held over their heads; symbolic of the mystery of love, shrouded and veiled from the prying light of day.

The couple headed to the altar: a bonfire. Two attendants followed, carrying a sieve filled with meal over the heads of the young couple; a sign of the plenty that would be in their house, and an omen of good luck and the blessing of children.

The ancient altar was a bonfire; and the couple went around it three times before getting wed. *Pagan Ireland*[2]

~ When the Bride goes from her seat to the altar, let the Bridesmaids close up the space on the seat quickly, lest her seat grow cold, and the Bride and Groom's love cool with it. *Germany*[3]

~ The couple walk around the altar three times to represent the Holy Trinity and to bring a blessing to their marriage. *Greece*

~ At the beginning of the wedding ceremony, the Bride 'Circles the Groom' seven times, symbolically creating the space that they will share as husband and wife. In Judaism, the number seven is mystical and represents completion and fulfilment. Just as the creation of the world was finished in seven days, so the seven circles complete the couple's search for each other. *Jewish*

~ Bride and Groom shall stand so close together that nobody can see through them. If at the altar they stand so far apart that you can see between them, they'll pull two ways. *Germany*[3]

~ Stand close together before the altar, lest witches creep in between you. *Germany*[3]

~ The Groom who sits ahead of his Bride during the wedding ceremony will be a hen-pecked husband. *The Philippines*

~ Bride and Groom should intertwine their hands at the ceremony so they will be joined together for always. *Ireland*

~ When a wedding pair joins hands before the altar, the one whose hand is coldest will die first. *Germany*[3]

~ During the wedding whichever of you has your hand above the other's, shall have the mastery within the marriage. *Germany*[3]

~ If the Bride pricks her finger during the service she will fall out with the Groom. *Russia*

~ If a Bride kneels on the Groom's cloak at the altar, she gets the upper hand. *Germany*[3]

~ Bats in a church during a wedding ceremony are a very bad omen.

~ A large rosary or white rope is wound around the couple's shoulders in a 'figure of eight' symbol of infinity, symbolising the couple's eternal union as one. *Spain*

~ Of a wedded pair, the one that first rises from the altar will die first. *Germany* [3]

~ The kiss is a way for the newlyweds to transfer a part of themselves into each other's souls and enable a way for their spirit to dwell in their spouse eternally.

~ A husked coconut is split as the newlyweds descend from the pedestal. The manner in which the coconut halves fall apart predicts the couple's total number of children, and what their sexes will be. *Sri Lanka*

~ To ensure a loving home and marriage, both Bride and Groom must join hands and jump over a broom laid on the floor. *South Africa*

~ To couple should walk through an archway of swords following the ceremony to ensure safe passage into their new life together.

The Wedding Rings

~ A wedding ring is a circle: an ancient symbol of eternity and completion.

~ The River Nile was the bringer of all fortune and life to the Egyptians, and the first wedding rings were made from plants such as rushes and reeds growing on its banks to bring fortune and life to the couple. *Ancient Egypt*

~ Egyptian gold, before the introduction of coinage, was usually kept in the form of a ring; and the Egyptian at his marriage placed one of these pieces of gold on his wife's finger to symbolise he was entrusting her with all his property. *Ancient Egypt* [19]

~ A gold ring symbolises eternity, everlasting love and commitment within marriage. *Ancient Rome*

~ Ancient rings were forged of iron, to represent the strength of the

72

couple's love and to last forever like the marriage. Iron also warded off evil spirits. ***Early Roman***

~ Wedding rings were carved with two clasped hands to keep the marriage together. ***Ancient Rome***

~ The hole in the centre of the ring symbolises a gateway to things and events known and unknown.

~ Joseph and Mary's wedding ring was made of onyx or amethyst and was reputed to be able to perform miracles. ***Catholic Legend***

~ Very early rings had a carved key through which a woman was thought to be able to open her husband's heart.

~ It was bad luck (in some places even illegal) to be married with a ring made of anything other than gold. ***Ireland***

~ The claddagh ring is a popular wedding ring as it symbolises love, loyalty, and friendship. Worn on the right hand, with the heart facing inwards, it means the wearer's heart is unoccupied. Worn facing outwards, it indicates love is being considered. When worn on the left hand facing outward, it signifies that the wearer is seriously committed or married. ***Ireland***

~ Ensure the ring is a perfect fit, as a ring that is too tight brings painful jealousy or the stifling of one party by the other. If the ring is too loose, a parting of the ways through careless acts or forgetfulness is indicated.

~ Because any evil spirits would be shaken out of it when it fell, it was a good omen if the Groom dropped the wedding ring during the ceremony.

~ Dropping the ring before or during the service is very unlucky.

~ If the ring rolls onto a gravestone in the floor, it predicts an early death for one of the pair; the Bride if the person buried beneath the stone is a woman, the Groom if it is a man.

~ If the dropped ring rolls away from the altar steps, it is an extremely bad omen.

~ A dropped ring predicts that the marriage will not be happy for long. *Russia & Philippines*

~ If the Groom drops the wedding ring during the ceremony, the marriage is doomed.

~ If either the Bride or Groom drops the ring, he or she will be the first of the pair to die.

~ If a guest touches the rings during the service they will get married soon themselves. *Russia*

~ It is very unlucky to remove the ring once it has been put on in church. If it falls off, or is accidentally removed, then the husband must replace it to avert the evil.

~ If either partner removes the ring for whatever reason, one of them will soon be unfaithful.

~ Premature removal of the ring foreshadows the destruction of the marriage, death of the husband or loss of his affection.

~ In some districts, it is thought safe to take your wedding ring off after the birth of your first child, but never before. *UK*

~ To lose a wedding ring foretells a break-up.

~ Whoever loses the wedding ring first, will die first. *Germany* [3]

~ The wedding ring's loss or breakage predicts the destruction of the marriage, through the death of the spouse, the loss of their affection, or some other disaster. *Europe*

~ Hang your wedding ring from a strand of your hair. Rub the ring up and down your index finger a couple of times and then hold it above the top of your outstretched right hand. The number of times the ring swings around in a circle before stopping will predict how many children you'll have.

~ If a suspended wedding ring swings in a circle over a pregnant woman's belly, she's having a girl, and if it swings back and forth, she's having a boy.

~ Rings are amulets against demons, witches, and ghosts. A woman in childbirth should never take off her wedding ring, as spirits and witches will then have power over her. ***Austrian Tyrol***[14]

~ Rub a baby's tooth or gum with Mum's gold wedding ring to ease his teething discomfort. ***Yorkshire: UK***

Leaving The Ceremony Area

~ Immediately the service is over, the newlyweds should look in the same mirror as each other for luck. ***Russia***

~ The husband should break a glass for luck immediately after the marriage ceremony. ***Turkey***

~ Directly the wedding is over, the strongest of the guests lifts the Bride and Groom aloft to heighten their marital bliss. ***Estonia***[3]

~ The Mother-in-law takes the Bride aside, unveils her, and with a pair of scissors cuts off the tips of her hair. This drives away all evil influences that might do harm or enter between the newly married pair. ***Tunisian Jews***[20]

~ Two white doves are set free to symbolise love and happiness for the wedded pair. ***Armenia***

~ The release of doves wards off evil spirits.

~ Friends and relatives wash the feet of both the Bride and Groom, to prepare them to set off on a new and clean path. *Scotland*

~ People were spat on to secure health and a long life. *Ireland*

~ Spittle is 'soul-stuff' and is lucky, often used for healing and warding off evil spirits. Therefore the onlookers may spit on the Bride and Groom for luck. *Islamic Nations*

~ Spit three times on the couple for luck. *Asia*

~ Whenever someone compliments the Bride, she or her family must knock on unpolished wood or spit three times over their left shoulder to chase off any evil. *Russia*

~ After admiring the couple, people must spit to avoid accidentally giving them the 'evil eye.' *Italy*

~ Care is taken to not mention the good health of the couple, lest any human or spirit becomes jealous and makes them ill. *Vietnam*

~ Never say good words about the newlyweds as evil spirits will hear them and may want to harm the couple as a result. *Kyrgyzstan*

~ The young couple run out of church, hand in hand at top speed to secure rapid progress in their business. *Estonia* [3]

~ As the couple exit Church, the one who keeps quiet for the longest will be the boss within the marriage. *Russia*

~ The couple should toss coins to the crowd as they leave the church for luck. *Scotland*

~ If you catch a candy which is thrown by the Bride, you will wed in a short period of time. *Turkey*

~ As the Bride exits the church, onlookers break an egg to grant her many children with easy labours each time. *Russia*

~ Breaking a coconut, pottery or an egg against a wall while facing

Mecca are all considered symbolic of the hymen breaking leading to conception. The noise also confuses evil spirits, stopping them from harming the Bride's fertility. *India, Russia & Iraq*

~ An unmarried woman who literally follows the footsteps of the newlyweds will marry soon. *The Philippines*

~ No one should cross the road before the couple.

~ The Bride and Groom are blessed, and all those who touch them will receive good luck and fortune.

~ A man should always be the first to wish joy to the Bride, never a woman as that is unlucky. *Ireland*

~ The common greeting to a new Bride among some tribes is, 'May thou bear twelve children with him.' *Africa*

~ The moon is particularly associated with fertility. Therefore, it's customary to call out after newlyweds, 'Increase, O Moon.' *Sweden*[4]

~ If the newlyweds first meet a girl after they leave the Church, their first child will be a daughter; if a boy, a son; if a boy and girl together, they will have twins. *Germany*[3]

~ It is unlucky for a married couple to meet a white horse first thing after their wedding. *Ireland*

~ Ducks or a goose and gander are included in the wedding processional to symbolise fidelity as they all mate for life. *Japan*

~ The Bride must not come out by a Church gate through which a corpse has been recently carried out. *UK*

Confetti

~ Variations to throwing coloured paper confetti throughout the world include throwing nuts, grains, flowers, petals, bread, cakes, sugared almonds, red dates, figs, raisins, eggs or salt.

~ Throwing confetti is a relic of former fertility rites. A couple were showered with grain and nuts (life-giving seeds) to transfer the seeds' fertility onto the couple. *Pagan*

~ The walnut was associated with Juno, the goddess of women and marriage. Walnuts were therefore thrown at the Bride and Groom for fertility. *Ancient Rome*

~ The hazel nut is a symbol of life. *Celtic*

~ Nuts have long been used as fertility charms. *Romany Gypsy*

~ As grains and nuts representing new life and plenty were thrown at the Newlyweds, onlookers shouted, 'Be fertile and increase!' *Jewish* [13]

~ The Groom's parents throw nuts and plums to a Bride. If the Bride picks up some nuts, she'll have many sons. *Korea*

~ Nuts were offered to the Bride and Groom as they left the church as fertility blessings. *Ancient Rome*

~ As a Bride leaves Church, an elderly woman presents her with a little bag containing hazel nuts to enhance her fertility. *Devon: UK*

~ 'To go a-nutting' is a euphemism for love-making; and the saying goes that a year in which are plenty of nuts will also be one in which many children will be born. *Cornwall: UK*

~ While the couple are still kneeling at the foot of the altar, a rain of nuts is poured over their heads and down their backs. *France* [6]

~ A handful of sand was scattered before the Bride & Groom to echo the promise given to Abraham, the Father of the Jews, 'I will make your descendants as numerous as the grains of sand on the seashore.' *Jewish*

~ Throwing rice confetti at the newlyweds will bring them lifelong prosperity. *Philippines*

~ Corn was thrown in the newlyweds faces with cries of 'abundance' or 'plenty' to bring them prosperity. *Medieval Europe*[6]

~ Red beads are tossed at Newlyweds to bring them good luck. *Mexico*

CHAPTER 7

THE WEDDING RECEPTION

FOOD

~ It's usual to fast from food while marrying. Those who fail to fast without mighty motives will only get mute children. **France** [1]

~ As the (unlucky) 'Last Supper' was celebrated upstairs by Jesus and his disciples, all meals must take place on the ground floor for luck.

~ Garlic or onion bulbs should be hung up in the corners of the room to ward off vampires and other evil spirits. **Europe**

~ Garlic magically protects against poison and sorcery. According to Pliny, this is because when it's hung up in the open air for a time, it turns black. It's thus believed to be attracting evil into itself away from the wearer or householder. **Ancient Rome**

~ Food should be scattered at the doors and under the tables to placate the jinn (evil spirits). **Islamic**

~ After the feast, ensure you leave a little food out for the fairies or you will offend them and they will get you back. **Ireland**

~ The floor of the room where the wedding breakfast is to be held is strewn with nuts as fertility charms. **Poitou: France**

~ Two swords were stuck into the wall over where the Bride and Groom sat during the wedding feast; the one whose sword kept up the longest vibration lived the longest. **Estonia** [3]

~ At the marriage feast they set two candles before the Bride and Groom; the one whose light went out first all by itself was sure to die first. **Estonia** [3]

~ Newlyweds should be taken around a table representing their house three times. *Russia*

~ If the couple scrimp on their wedding feast, then their marital happiness will suffer as a consequence. They may even become infertile for their 'mean spiritedness'. *UK*

~ Couples should eat three mouthfuls of salt and oatmeal at the beginning of their wedding reception as protection against the power of the 'evil eye'. *Ireland*

~ At the wedding reception, a nine-course meal should be served as nine is a lucky and magical number. *China*

~ The Bride must avoid eating from the corner of a table as this causes problems with the in-laws and results in a wrecked marriage. *Indonesia*

~ Couples shared a quince to bring marital happiness. *Ancient Rome*

~ The couple share red dates to ensure a sweet life together. *Korea*

~ The Bride must eat sugar plums shaped like hazel nuts for her fertility. *Hautes-Alpes* [6]

~ The Groom's mother and father offer bread and salt to the new couple: the spouse who chooses the biggest piece of bread without using their hands will be the boss within the marriage. *Russia*

~ At the wedding reception, the parents of the Bride and Groom greet the newlyweds with bread, which is lightly sprinkled with salt and a glass of wine. The bread is given so that the couple will never hunger or be in need. The salt reminds the couple that their life may be difficult at times, and they must learn to cope with marriage's ups and downs. The wine is given so the couple will never thirst and have good health, happiness and good company. *Poland*

~ Some wedding bread should be saved so that the couple may not want. Such bread does not get mouldy, and a piece of it put in the pottage is good for the soon-to-be pregnant Bride if she has no appetite. **Germany**[3]

~ A Bride preserves her bridal wreath and a piece of wedding bread; so long as she keeps the hardened lump she'll never want for bread. When man and wife are weary of life, they eat the bread soaked in pottage. **Germany**[3]

~ The 'Best Man' cuts a small piece off a whole loaf, butters it, and puts it in the Bride's mouth. This is so the couple's children will have small, smooth mouths. **Estonia**[3]

~ Bread was placed in the bottom of two drinking glasses full of wine. The newlyweds drank this as fast as they could as the first person to get to the 'toast' ruled the marriage. **France**

~ White storks, pomegranates, fish, fowl, wheat and midwives were all popular illustrations on wedding pastries expressing the couple's wish for children. **Jewish**[13]

~ An engaged couple should not sit at the same table as the pair just married, nor even put their feet under it; else no end of mischief befalls one of the couples. **Germany**[3]

~ If two eat off one plate, they will become enemies. **Germany**[3]

~ If newlyweds eat with same spoon, they will not be satisfied with each other. **Russia**

~ At a wedding dinner let the butter dishes have been begun, or the bachelors there will all be rejected when they woo.

~ On no account should married people eat the house-cock. **Germany**[3]

~ Nothing green was permitted in the decorations, and no green vegetables were served at the wedding feast. The reason being was that the fairies, whose chosen colour it is, would resent the insult and destroy the wearer. ***Scottish Lowlands***[6]

~ Five Sugared Almonds, representing Health, Wealth, Happiness, Fertility and Long Life are wrapped in ornamental materials and presented to all the female guests at the Wedding. ***Italy***

~ Bridesmaids should not wash the dishes or they will fall out with the married couple. ***Russia***

~ A Bride and Groom should never wash their hands in the same sink at the same time or disaster will befall them. ***Ireland***

Drink

~ Honey wine called 'Bunratty Meade' is drunk at weddings to promote virility. Couples also drank it from special goblets for a month following the wedding, which is where the word 'honeymoon' comes from. As well as enhancing virility, honey wine was believed to be a defence against the fairies stealing the Bride away. ***Ireland***

~ At the meal they are wilfully wasteful of the beer, and spill it about, so that the couple will have a life of plenty. ***Estonia***[3]

~ Before a wedding, the Groom shall broach the beer-cask, and put the tap in his pocket, or bad people will do him a mischief. ***Germany***[3]

~ The Bride and Groom must observe the tap of their first beer or wine cask at their reception for luck. ***Germany***[3]

~ Coins should be put in the couple's glasses. These coins should be then taken home and put underneath the tablecloth to bring wealth to their household. ***Russia***

~ Two bottles of champagne are tied together and kept, so that the couple may celebrate their first anniversary with the birth of their first child. *Russia*

~ A lucky bottle of champagne from the reception is saved to 'wet the baby's head' at the christening. *Ireland*

~ If the Bride spills something red on her dress, then it is prophesying that she is a 'stained bride' and has not told the truth about her sexual history to her husband.

~ If a Bride spills something at the reception, her husband will become a drunk. *Russia*

~ The health of the Bride must be toasted in wine, spirits or beer. To drink her health in a 'soft' drink brings her lots of bad luck. *Ireland*

~ Clink the glasses you use when toasting; this way, the glasses are never used for a better purpose.

~ Traditional wedding steins had acorn shaped thumb-lifts, the acorn being symbolic of fertility. *Germany*

~ If glasses break at a wedding, the couple will never be rich. *Germany*[3]

~ It's bad luck if a glass or cup is broken on the wedding day. *Ireland*

~ Breaking something during the reception brings good luck to the newlyweds. *Philippines*

~ After the wedding, one of the Bridesmaids hurries home, gets beer or brandy, and offers a glass of it to the Groom, who empties the glass and tosses it behind his back. If the glass breaks, it's good luck; if it doesn't break it's bad luck. *Germany*[3]

The Wedding Cake

~ The wedding cake is a very ancient feature of the marriage feast, symbolising fertility and good fortune.

~ By tradition, the cake should be made of fine wheaten flour and of as rich a mixture as possible to indicate abundance and prosperity.

~ The wedding cake was originally made of flour, water and salt, and the couple ate it in a symbolical act to ensure that they would never know want. ***Ancient Rome***

~ The wedding cake was a multi-level fruitcake with a small cedar tree on top of it. This tree was later planted to flourish and grow with the love of the Bride and Groom. ***Bermuda***

~ The wedding cake is actually a fertility cake, as large, sweet cakes have long been associated with fertility. ***Roman Catholic***

~ Early wedding cakes were flat and round, containing fruit and nuts symbolising fertility. ***UK***

~ The shape of the modern three tiered cake symbolises the spire of St. Bride's Church in the City of London. ***UK***

~ Icing made of white sugar and bitter almonds is symbolic of the fluctuations of pleasure and pain that come with any marriage. ***UK***

~ Traditionally, the bottom layer of a wedding cake represents the couple as a family, and the top layer represents them as a couple. Each layer in between represents a child that they will have.

~ The top tier should be an Irish whiskey cake, to be saved for the christening of the couple's first baby. ***Ireland***

~ The first slice of wedding cake must always be cut by the Bride; otherwise the marriage will be childless.

~ The Bride and the Groom must make the first cut in the cake together, to ensure a happy shared future. The couple should then cut a slice and share it between them. Smashing the wedding cake into your new spouse's face symbolises that you will 'feed' and take care of each other throughout your marriage.

~ Everyone present must eat a piece of cake. To refuse is very unlucky, both for the bridal pair and for the person concerned.

~ To refuse to eat a piece of wedding cake wishes ill on the Bride.

~ Sending pieces of wedding cake to friends not present on the day, stems from the wish that they will share in the cake's luck-bringing properties too.

~ The Bride should keep a portion of the wedding cake, so her husband will stay faithful to her forever.

~ The Bridesmaids should place their slice of wedding cake under their pillows that night so that they will dream of their future husbands. *Scotland*

~The Bride holds her wedding ring between the forefinger and thumb of her right hand, through which the Groom passes each portion of the cake a magic nine times. A Bridesmaid should seal up her portion of cake in a pretty envelope, deposit it in the foot of her left stocking, and place it under her pillow when she goes to bed so that she may dream of her future husband. *England*

~ A single person should take a piece of wedding cake and pass it between three and nine times through a wedding ring, then they should sleep on it to dream the face of their future spouse. *Ireland*[2]

~ Place a ring in the cake. The guest who finds the ring in their slice of cake will be ensured happiness throughout the next year. *UK*

~ There were usually three wedding cakes; one main wedding cake, and two smaller cakes called 'The Bride's Cake' and 'The Groom's Cake'. Baked into these cakes were little charms; a ring, a penny, a thimble, and a button. Each charm held its own meaning:

> *'The ring for marriage within a year;*
>
> *The penny for wealth, my dear;*
>
> *The thimble for an old maid or bachelor born;*
>
> *The button for sweethearts all forlorn.'* **Victorian UK**

~ At weddings, beside the great cake, they make a bachelor's cake, which the girls pull to pieces. She who gets the largest piece will get a husband first. **Germany** [3]

~ The wedding cake was originally made from many small wheat cakes (in Scotland, oat cakes) that were broken over the Bride's head to bless her fertility. This evolved to crumbling or breaking the cake over the Bride's head. **UK**

~ A plate of cake was flung over the Bride's head as she left the church, and omens were read from the way the plate broke. The more pieces there were, the happier the marriage would be. In some places, the number of broken bits indicated the number of children the couple would have. If the plate remained intact, it was a bad sign, and then it was rapidly stamped on to avert the evil. The cake itself was scrambled for by the guests and torn into luck-bringing fragments. **Yorkshire: UK**

~ A similar custom was observed with shortbread. Here the scramble and the omen reading took place when the married pair reached their new home. **Scotland**

~ If the Bride's mother-in-law breaks a piece of wedding cake on the

Bride's head as she enters the house after the ceremony, they will be friends for life. ***Ireland***

~ On her return from church, meet the Bride with cake cut into slices; every guest should take a slice and push it against the Bride's body for luck. ***Germany***[3]

The Entertainment at the Wedding Reception

~ It's bad luck for a Bride or the Groom to sing at their own wedding. ***Ireland***

~ When the couple are dancing, the Bride must not take both her feet off the floor as the fairies will then gain the upper hand. Fairies love beautiful things and one of their favourite things is a Bride. They may well kidnap her. ***Ireland***

~ At wedding feasts it was usual when dancing to 'dance for flax', that is, the higher the feet were raised from the floor, the higher the host's crop of flax at the next harvest would be. ***German Pennsylvania***[21]

~ As the couple dance, banknotes are stuck/tucked onto the Bride's garments for luck. ***Greece***

~ The Bride and Groom dance around Poitou's large walnut tree so the Bride may produce an abundance of milk for her babies. ***France***

~ A traditional folk song called 'Twelve Angels' is played at the reception, allowing the Bride to transfer her veil, and good luck to be married, to first her Maid of Honor, then her Bridesmaids, then her Flower Girl. ***Poland***

~ No separate wedding photos should be taken of the couple, as if so, they will fall apart. ***Russia***

~ Avoid taking pictures with odd numbers of people present as this means the quick death of one of the people in the photo. *Indonesia*

~ All fighting must be avoided at a wedding; as a quarrel is considered a most unlucky omen. *Ireland* [2]

Wedding Presents

~ At the close of a wedding breakfast, a servant carries about a plate containing salt, upon which the guests place money for luck. *Pomerania*[4]

~ It's bad luck to give away any wedding present.

~ Giving a wooden spoon blesses the new Bride's cooking skills.

~ Knives and other sharp and pointed objects are a bad choice for wedding gifts as they will lead to a broken marriage. *Philippines*

~ The Groom presents his Bride with an engraved silver teaspoon on their wedding day to symbolise that they will never go hungry. *Scotland*

~ Giving a bell as a wedding gift is traditional as the chime of bells keeps evil spirits away, restores harmony if a couple is fighting, and reminds a couple of their wedding vows. *Ireland*

~ Giving an *arinola* (chamber-pot) as a wedding gift brings good luck to the newlyweds. *Philippines*

~ A black cat as a wedding present brings good luck to the Bride. *Midlands: UK*

~ Salt and bread, representing the necessaries of life, are the first articles given and then taken into the newlyweds' home. *Russia*[4]

~ For good luck, the newlyweds are given a horseshoe to display in their home with the prongs pointing in an upward position.

~ A pine tree, symbolic of luck and fertility, is planted outside the couple's home as a wedding present. ***Holland & Switzerland***

~ Two small pine trees are placed on either side of the Newlywed's front door until they have a baby. ***Norway***

~ Mango leaves are given to bless the couple with sons. ***India***

~ Friends plant a tree at the couple's new home and decorate it with ribbons and painted eggshells. Legend says the Bride will live as long as the tree. ***Czech Republic***

~ Wedding guests are given beautifully decorated hardboiled eggs, symbolic of the Newlyweds' wish for children. ***Malaysia***

~ Rose quartz is traditionally given to Brides to promote pregnancies and discourage miscarriages.

~ The Newlyweds are wrapped in a gift of a batik cloth called a 'selendang'. This symbolises the hope for the couple to have children, as the selendang is traditionally used to carry babies. ***Malaysia***

~ Terracotta elephants are traditional wedding gifts, as elephants are associated with rain, which makes the fields fertile. ***India***

CHAPTER 8

HEADING INTO MARRIED LIFE

Tying Shoes to the Car

~ The shoe is an ancient symbol in many countries of life, liberty, and entire personal control.

~ It was in the sense of confirming a sale or exchange that the Jews understood the removal and giving of a shoe or sandal. So the Bride, who was originally always a slave, transferred herself by the symbol of the shoe. [10]

~ When the Emperor Waldimir made proposals of marriage to the daughter of Ragnald, she replied scornfully that she would not take off her shoes to the son of a slave. Gregory of Tours, in speaking of wedding, says the Groom, having given a ring to the Bride, 'presents her with a shoe.'

~ The shoes and sandals of the Greeks, Romans, Egyptians, and Jews were ornamented with horns, crescents, and other representations of the moon, while at marriage ceremonies the custom of casting the shoe was, and is now, combined with the throwing of flowers and various kinds of grain. These symbols and offerings seem to indicate the propitiation of a god, probably the deity who presided over productiveness. [10]

~ The shoe is an ancient symbol of marriage and maidenly chastity, an idea also found both in Northern and Indian mythologies. [4.]

~ The Bride was symbolically struck with a shoe by her Groom to establish his authority. *Anglo-Saxon*

91

~ The casting of the old shoe signifies the surrender of authority by the Father of the Bride to the new husband.

~ The shoe is a symbol of life, especially as shown in fertility. Hence old shoes are thrown after a Bride, the Jewish crying, 'Increase and multiply'.

> *'There was an old woman who lived in a shoe,*
>
> *Who had so many children she didn't know what to do.'*

This nursery rhyme can be traced back to this early mythology. [18]

~ Guests threw shoes at the Bride and Groom, and the couple would have great luck if they or their carriage were hit. ***Tudor England***

~ An old shoe must be thrown over the Bride's head as she leaves the Church to bring her luck. ***Ireland***

~ Old shoes are thrown after the Bride and Groom so any old and worn memories will depart. ***Russia***

~ Brides threw shoes at their Bridesmaids to see who would marry next.

~ Throwing shoes after the couple brings luck, especially in making journeys. Ben Johnson wrote, 'Hurl after me a shoe, I'll be merry whatever I'll do,' and old Heywood says, 'And home again hitherward quick as a bee, Now for good luck, cast an old shoe at me;' while Tennyson tells us, 'And wheresoe'er thou move, good luck, Shall throw her old shoe after.' [10]

Returning Home

~ The wedding party should always take the longest route home from Church. ***Ireland***

~ The couple must return by a different route to which they arrived.

~ When the Bride goes home, she should not make a circuit, but go the common road; or she will have bad luck. ***Germany*** [3]

~ Water should be poured after the wedding car so the Bride will not return to her mother's home. ***Turkey***

~ The Bride is carefully guarded by women on her way to the Groom's place as they fear a witch or warlock may somehow magically deprive the Bride of her virginity en-route. ***Morocco*** [14]

~ If a shepherd drives his sheep in the way of the Bride on her way home, she should give the shepherd some money, and she'll have good luck. ***Germany*** [3]

~ The Bride should arrive at the Groom's house in the dark: then the couple will have every corner of their house full. ***Germany*** [3]

~ *'No Bride shall move in when the moon's on the wane; but wealth she will win, who comes riding through rain.'* [3]

~ The Bride should throw some flax away on her way home, so that the flax in the district will thrive. ***Germany*** [3]

~ Milk is offered to the Bride on her way to the Groom's place; she should dip her finger into it or drink a few drops and then blow on the rest to impart some of her 'holiness' to it. The milk is then either mixed with other milk to serve as a charm against witchcraft, poured into the churn to make the butter plentiful or sprinkled over the people for luck. ***Malaysia*** [14]

~ In bringing the young wife into the husband's house, they pull down the fence on both sides of the entrance, that she may drive in swiftly without hindrance. Then her pregnancies, labours & post-partum recoveries will be quick and easy. ***Estonia*** [3]

~ The Bride's father, just before she leaves to live with her husband, takes some white kaolin symbolising fertility passed on from his ancestors, and rubs it onto his daughter's stomach to bless her fertility. *Congo* [22]

~ The Bride hurls a lamb over the Groom's tent so that there will be many sheep in the village. *Muslim Malaysia* [14]

~ Boiling water should be poured over the threshold before a Bride enters her new home. *Scotland*

~ If, on coming home from church, the Bride is the first to take hold of the house door, she will maintain the mastery, especially if she says: 'This door I seize upon, here all my will be done!' If the Groom hears the spell, he may undo it by adding the words: 'I grasp this knocker ring, be fist and mouth (word and deed) one thing!' *Germany* [3]

~ Unless a Bride enters her new home first, domestic strife is bound to ensue. *Germany* [4]

~ Two Brides should never be brought into the same house. *Turkey*

~ The Bride is met on the threshold by the Groom's mother, who breaks an oaten cake (in Scotland, shortbread) over her head so the married couple will never know want and have plenty. *Ireland* [2]

~ The new Bride must enter her home by the main door, and must not trip or fall.

~ Tripping over the threshold was considered a bad omen so the Bride was lifted over it to prevent this. *Ancient Rome*

~ The Bride is carried over the threshold to protect her from the evil spirits who lurk under a house's threshold.

~ Thresholds are the dwelling place of the domovoi spirit, a temperamental brownie who protects the household. Letting a cat into the house with the newlyweds placates a domovoi and also brings riches. ***Russia***

~ The Groom must enter the house with his right foot first to bring good luck to the couple. ***Ancient Rome***

~ An unlocked door lock should be placed on the threshold; once the couple have entered the house they should lock this and throw it away. ***Russia***

~ To have a lucky married life and to prevent being bewitched, a married couple should step over a broom on first entering their house.

~ So the couple will not fall apart, the Bride must break a plate on first entering the house. ***Russia***

~ A Bride must bring the title-page of an astrological almanac into her new home along with other exorcising objects to protect her from evil. ***China***

~ When a Bride enters her new home, she should pick up seven silver dishes off the floor as quietly as possible, as the more noise she makes, the greater the number of fights will occur between the couple.

~ It's lucky if the Bride places dough on the door of her house, symbolising that she will be the housekeeper from now on.

~ The moment the Bride enters the house, she is led through every part of the house and grounds; and must drop ribbons or money into each part, even into the well and the fire, for the sake of her husband's happiness. ***Estonia*** [3]

~ Both sets of parents carry some fire from the hearths of their own homes to the newlywed's home to bring them luck and warmth. ***South Africa***

~ As soon as the couple have stepped into the house, a watchman must stay a good while by the household fire, so that no stranger may come near it and contrive to put an evil spell on the couple. *Estonia* [3]

~ Rowan and St. John's Wort protect from evil spirits and should be hung over the doorway of the newlyweds' new home. *UK*

~ A branch of the rowan tree was placed over the door, after being waved around while chanting the words, 'Avaunt, Satan!' *Northern Scotland*

~ Rosemary planted by the door keeps witches away. *UK*

~ Scatter primroses before the door, for the fairies can't pass the flowers. *Ireland*

~ A branch of aloe protects against spiritual intruders. *Egypt*

The Honeymoon Suite

~ Tie a red thread across the door to prevent the fairies entering and marring the couple's happiness. *Ireland*

~ A bowl of primroses somewhere in the room offers protection against witchcraft.

~ A honeymoon bed sheet should be blue to ensure the husband's virility and the granting of future sons. *Mexico*

~ Openings in pillowcases should touch each other to ensure marital happiness. *Russia*

~ If a pillow fall off the bridal bed, the one that lay on it will die first. *Germany* [3]

~ In Cyprus, a chubby baby boy is rolled up and down the marital bed before the wedding night so the couple will be blessed with boys. In the Czech Republic, a baby is similarly laid on the bed to bless the marriage with children.

~ The Godmothers help in making the bridal bed, the straws are put in one by one, and care is taken that no stranger enters the room. The bed must not be beaten, but softly stroked, else the wife will be beaten by her husband. *Germany*[3]

~ If feathers picked up between two fields are put in a marital bed, the man and wife will part. *Germany*[3]

~ A woman still producing breast milk should prepare the marital bed to encourage the newlyweds' fertility. *Scotland*

~ A hen that was a prolific layer was tied to the bed on the first night in the hope its fertility would be passed onto the couple. *Ireland*

~ The marital bed is traditionally arranged by an elderly couple who leave symbols of fertility such as rice and sesame seeds between its sheets. *Thailand*

The Hammer of Thor (Mjölner) is the symbol for Thor, the god of thunder and lightning, who was the friend and protector of all humans. According to legend, the hammer was forged by dwarves knowledgeable in magic and brought to Asgård, the home of the gods, as a gift to Thor. The hammer symbol stands for protection against evil forces and is a fertility symbol. Hammer symbols were put in the bed of newlyweds to protect their fertility. *Sweden*[23]

~ The couple's parents often tucked a fish between the newlyweds' sheets to ensure fertility. ***Oriental Jewish***

~ The Scottish place a willow branch beneath the newlyweds' bed to promote pregnancies. Pagans place a broom.

~ Newlyweds must get into bed together at the same time. ***Germany***[3]

~ If the Bride gets into bed first, and makes the Groom hand her a glass of water, she is sure to be master of the marriage. ***Germany***[3]

~ Candles near the beds drive away spirits. ***Medieval Europe***

~ In the Bride chamber let the light burn quite clean out rather than snuff it out. ***Germany***[3]

~ Whoever goes to sleep first on the wedding night, will die first and whoever gets out of bed first will die first. ***Germany & Estonia***[3]

The Honeymoon

~ As the blood of the hymen was greatly feared, the Best Man was sometimes expected to consummate the marriage on behalf of the groom, to ensure no bad luck or evil spirits could destroy the couple's fertility.

~ The virgin Bride should first be deflowered by a stone phallus symbolising the god Shiva. Then a fertile marriage will result. ***India***

~ The word 'Honeymoon' originates from the times when the man captured his Bride and hid her from her parents for one 'moon' cycle (month). During that time the couple drank a mixture of honey and wine, to increase their fertility.

~ Friends of the Newlyweds' burst into the bridal chamber and offered the couple soup from the chamber pot to give them strength and fertility. ***Languedoc: France***

~ The couple must be careful not to break anything while on their honeymoon, especially a mirror.

~ Occasional quarrels during the honeymoon ensure a harmonious and happy future.

~ The Bride may now wear green, as it will now bring her good fortune and much love at this time.

~ The evil powers that come out at Samhain (Halloween) lived the rest of the time in the cave of Cruachan in Connaught. This cave was called the 'hell-gate of Ireland,' and was unlocked on November Eve to let out spirits and copper-coloured birds which killed the farm animals and stole Brides. Therefore, newlyweds must be very careful to guard against abduction at this time. ***Ireland***[2]

~ If she wishes to tame a bad-tempered husband, the Bride's first care is to prepare for him a soup made with the rain-water of a Friday's shower.[4]

~ The first partner to buy a new item after the wedding will be the dominant one in the relationship. For this reason, many Brides ensure that they make the first purchase by arranging to buy a small item such as a pin from the Chief Bridesmaid immediately after the ceremony.

~ If the Groom sneezes when he gets up in the morning, he should lie down again for another three hours, or his wife will be master of the marriage for one week. ***Germany***[3]

~ If another couple's baby's first trip out-of-doors is to visit newlyweds, the newlyweds will soon have a baby of their own. ***German Pennsylvania USA***

Fertility Related Rites

~ The word 'Bride' is derived from the name 'St. Bridget', who was the Christian version of the Irish Goddess of Fertility, Brid. *Ireland*

~ A red string is tied around the Bride's body; and when the wedding is over, she must breathe out until she breaks the string. This ritual is sure to prevent difficult births in the future for her. *Estonia* [3]

~ The Groom threw a fish at his Bride's feet in a fertility rite. *Libyan Jews* [2]

~ A Bride jumps over a platter with a large fish on it, to shouts of blessing such as, 'may you multiply like fish'. *Jewish Custom from The Balkans* [2]

~ During the marriage fertility rite known as 'pouring water on the hands,' the Bride and Groom's little fingers of their right hands are tied together with a white thread. The father of the Bride then ritualistically pours water, a symbol of fertility, from a golden pitcher onto the thread. *Sri Lanka*

~ If a cat sneezes near the Bride on her wedding day, it will bring her good luck and fertility.

~ A broom used at the wedding ceremony brings fertility. *Pagan*

~ During the Middle Ages and down to the Eighteenth Century, it was commonly believed that the consummation of a marriage could be prevented by anyone who, while the wedding ceremony was taking place, either locked a lock or tied a knot in a cord, and then threw the lock or the cord away. The lock or the knotted cord had to be flung into water; and until it was found and unlocked or untied, no real union of the couple was possible.

Therefore, it was a grave offence, not only to cast such a spell, but also to steal the lock or knotted cord. In the year 1718, the parliament of Bordeaux sentenced someone to be burned alive for having spread desolation through a whole family by means of knotted cords; and in Scotland in 1705, two people were condemned to death for stealing charmed knots which a woman had made to mar the wedded happiness of Spalding of Ashintilly. [15]

~ To render a Groom impotent, an enchanter ties a knot in a handkerchief which he secretes on some part of the Groom's body: so long as the knot in the handkerchief remains tied, the Groom remains impotent. **North Africa** [15]

Notes

[1] John George Hohman, 'Pow-Wows', PA, USA, 1820

[2] Lady Francesca Speranza Wilde, 'Ancient Legends, Mystic Charms, and Superstitions of Ireland' London: Ward & Downey, 1887

[3] Robert Mearns Lawrence, 'The Magic Of The Horseshoe with other Folklore Notes', Boston And New York, Houghton, Mifflin & Co., 1898

[4] Vide Grimm's 'Teutonic Mythology', translated into English and kindly used by permission of The Northvegr Foundation www.norvegr.com

[5] Walter E. Roth, 'An Inquiry into the Animism and Folklore of the Guyana Indians' from the Thirtieth Annual Report of the Bureau of American Ethnology, 1908-1909, pp. 103-386, Washington D.C., 1915

[6] Sabine Baring-Gould, 'A Book Of Folklore', London: Collins, 1913

[7] Lafcadio Hearn, 'New Orleans Superstitions' from *An American miscellany*, vol. II, (1924) originally published in *Harper's weekly*, 1886

[8] R. O. Winstedt, 'Shaman, Saiva and Sufi, A Study of the Evolution of Malay Magic', Constable & Company Ltd, 1925

[9] Thanks to Sigurd Towrie at www.orkneyjar.com

[10] Thomas Firminger Thiselton-Dyer, 'Folklore of Women as illustrated by legendary and traditionary tales, folk rhymes, proverbial sayings, superstitions etc' London: Elliot Stock, 1906

[11] Eli Edward Burriss, 'Taboo, Magic, Spirits: A Study of Primitive Elements in Roman Religion' New York, Macmillan Company, 1931

[12] T. Sharper Knowlson, 'The Origins of Popular Superstitions and Customs,' 1910

[13] Michelle Klein, 'A Time to Be Born,' The Jewish Publication Society, PA, 2001

[14] Sir James George Frazer, 'The Golden Bough, A Study of Magic and Religion', Abridged Edition, 1922

[15] Samuel M. Zwemer F.R.G.S. 'The Influence of Animism on Islam: An Account of Popular Superstitions' 1913

[16] William Cashen, 'Manx Folklore', Douglas G. & L. Johnson, 1912.

[17] Robert Hunt, 'The Drolls, Traditions and Superstitions of Old Cornwall (Popular Romances of the West of England)' 2nd ed. London: John Camden Hotten, 1871

[18] Charles Godfrey Leland 'Gypsy Sorcery And Fortune Telling' London: T Fisher Unwin, 1891

[19] Samuel Sharpe, 'Egyptian Mythology and Egyptian Christianity', London, J.R. Smith, 1863

[20] Frederick Thomas Elworthy, 'The Evil Eye - An Account of this Ancient and Widespread Superstition' London: J. Murray; 1895

[21] W. J. Hoffman, M. D. 'Folklore of the Pennsylvania Germans' Part I: Journal of American Folk-Lore 1:2 1888, Part II: Journal of American Folk-Lore 2:4 , 1889

[22] Hermann Hochegger (Ed), 'Encyclopedia of Ritual Symbolics' (R. D. Congo). Ceeba publications, Antenne d'Autriche. St. Gabriel, Mödling, 2004.

[23] Thanks to Ulf Holmberg of Ulfie's Forge, a master blacksmith who makes these and other wonderful items, see www.uffes-smedja.nu

Printed in the United Kingdom
by Lightning Source UK Ltd.
104774UKS00001BA/6